CREATION AT RISK?

MICHAEL CROMARTIE is a senior fellow and director of the Evangelical Studies Project at the Ethics and Public Policy Center in Washington, D.C. He is the co-editor, with Richard John Neuhaus, of *Piety and Politics: Evangelicals and Fundamentalists Confront the World*, and the editor of *Disciples and Democracy: Religious Conservatives and the Future of American Politics*, and other volumes.

CREATION AT RISK?

Religion, Science, and Environmentalism

Edited by
MICHAEL CROMARTIE

Essays by Thomas S. Derr ▪ Gregg Easterbrook
Peter J. Hill ▪ Patrick J. Michaels
Charles T. Rubin ▪ *and others*

ETHICS AND PUBLIC POLICY CENTER
WASHINGTON, D.C.

WILLIAM B. EERDMANS PUBLISHING COMPANY
GRAND RAPIDS, MICHIGAN / CAMBRIDGE, U.K.

Published jointly 1995 by the Ethics and Public Policy Center and
Wm. B. Eerdmans Publishing Co.
255 Jefferson Ave. S.E., Grand Rapids, Michigan 49503 /
P.O. Box 163, Cambridge CB3 9PU U.K.

Printed in the United States of America

01 00 99 98 97 96 95 7 6 5 4 3 2 1

Library of Congress Cataloging-in-Publication Data

Creation at risk? religion, science, and environmentalism /
edited by Michael Cromartie; essays by Thomas Sieger Derr . . . and others.
p. cm.
Papers from a conference held in Nov. 1994.
Includes bibliographical references and index.
ISBN 0-8028-4104-X (paper: alk. paper)
1. Nature — Religious aspects — Congresses. 2. Environmentalism — Congresses.
I. Cromartie, Michael. II. Derr, Thomas Sieger, 1931- .
BL65.N35C74 1995
363.7 — dc20 95-44384
CIP

Contents

Preface

April 1995 marked the twenty-fifth anniversary of Earth Day, and religious leaders of nearly every stripe joined in the effort to keep Americans aware of the damage mankind has inflicted upon the environment. Roman Catholic, mainline Protestant, evangelical, Jewish, and Orthodox clerics and theologians exhorted their constituencies to become better stewards of God's creation.

The extent of the problem is an area of hot dispute. Environmental scientists disagree about the meaning of the scientific data, and the effectiveness of public policies and regulations intended to ensure clean air, clean water, and the conservation of our natural resources is a matter of considerable controversy among political scientists and economists. Attitudes in society range from those who see environmental doomsday fast approaching to those who say there is no serious problem.

In November 1994 the Ethics and Public Policy Center's Evangelical Studies Project brought together a diverse group of scholars and practitioners from a range of disciplines to explore some of the scientific, religious, philosophical, moral, economic, and political claims now afloat in the environmental movement. For a day and a half the participants engaged in a lively and stimulating exchange centered on papers presented by four academic experts: Charles T. Rubin, associate professor of political science at Duquesne University; Thomas Sieger Derr, professor of religion and biblical literature at Smith College; Patrick J. Michaels, associate professor of environmental science at the University of Virginia; and Peter J. Hill, professor of economics at Wheaton College. Each paper was followed by a response by a distinguished commentator. This volume also includes pertinent comments made by a dozen other participants, in addition to the eight speakers. All are identified on pages 151-52. An additional essay by journalist Gregg Easterbrook draws upon his 1995 book on the environmental good news.

Charles Rubin argues that environmentalism needs to be recognized as a distinct ideology. Environmentalists believe that "everything is connected to everything else," and that man's relationship to fragile and endangered nature must be completely reformed. Because "the environment" is seen as all-inclusive, the solutions most environmentalists advocate tend to be global, utopian, and totalitarian in character. "Such visions," argues Rubin, "make the best the enemy of the better, creating dissatisfaction with everything we have achieved or indeed could possibly achieve." He proposes that rather than trying to "save the earth" or "plan it for the planet," responsible citizens should take grassroots action to solve specific environmental problems at the local level. Respondent **Andrew Kimbrell**, an attorney and bioethicist, strongly disagrees with Rubin about "the roots and the problems of environmentalism" and charges him with describing a "Greenenstein" environmental monster that doesn't really exist.

Patrick Michaels reviews some of the scientific issues at the heart of environmentalism. Concerns about "global warming" have energized the movement, but Michaels argues that current data do not support the dire predictions about climate change publicized widely in the late 1980s. Ignoring the disparities between computer forecasts and observable temperatures has led, he says, to the adoption of ineffective and expensive public policies. Such policies undermine responsible environmentalism and create a "great deal of public distrust of science in general." Respondent **Christopher Flavin**, vice-president of the Worldwatch Institute, chides Michaels for having an unacceptable complacency about global warming. Our very "uncertainty" about the consequences of the buildup of greenhouse gases should cause us to take precautionary actions to minimize risks, Flavin says.

Gregg Easterbrook, a contributing editor to *Newsweek,* celebrates the "stunning success" of environmental legislation such as the Clean Air Act, the Clean Water Act, and the Endangered Species Act and faults environmental activists for continuing to promote "images of futility, crisis, and decline." He finds this way of thinking "an anachronism, rendered obsolete by its own success." **Ronald Bailey** in his response argues that Easterbrook "confuses the results of economic progress and wealth creation with the effects of environmental regulation" and therefore "fails to understand that the affluence created by free markets precedes and enables environmental cleanup."

Thomas Derr explores the theological implications of biocentrism. Biocentrists regard the Christian idea of stewardship as "repulsively anthropocentric, implying as it plainly does that human beings are in charge of nature, managing it for purposes that they alone are able to perceive." And since biocentrists believe that non-human and human life are of equal value and that both have rights, they object to man's running the show. Derr declares that nature is amoral and "has neither intrinsic value nor rights"; its value derives from its Creator, and rights must be confined to human beings, the only creatures capable of responsibility. Respondent **James Nash**, executive director of the Churches' Center for Theology and Public Policy, accuses Derr of falsifying the picture through "excessive generalizations" and "indiscriminate consolidation" of disparate groups. The moral claims of non-human life cannot be dismissed altogether, because nature, as God's creation, does have claims on us. We must learn, Nash observes, to be more "altruistic predators."

Peter J. Hill weighs the relative merits of markets and governments in dealing with ecological problems. Market failure is often used to justify government intervention, but Hill observes that government is hampered by similar shortcomings. The political process rewards perception more than substance and is easily twisted by special interests. Hill suggests that rather than focusing on collectivist solutions, government should work to improve our system of private property rights, which holds people "accountable for the actions they take that disadvantage others." Respondent **Andrew Steer**, director of the World Bank's environment department, agrees with Hill about the limitations of government but argues that a move toward private solutions would have to be tempered by attention to the common good. He recommends a "pragmatic approach" that "harnesses market power and uses coercion where necessary." He also suggests that U.S. environmental policy is less ineffective than it is inefficient.

I would like to thank several colleagues at the Ethics and Public

Policy Center. Carol Griffith, senior editor, did her usual masterful job of both editing the papers and retrieving the most important comments buried within the many pages of discussion transcript. Eric Owens helped organize the conference, transcribed the tapes, and typed the manuscript, all with good cheer and high competence. I am grateful to George Weigel, the president of the Ethics and Public Policy Center, for his encouragement and supportive leadership.

A very special thanks is extended to Howard and Roberta Ahmanson and to Victor Porlier for their generous support of the conference and the book.

"Disagreement is a rare achievement," said the great Jesuit scholar John Courtney Murray, "and most of what is called disagreement is simply confusion." At all our conferences it is our express purpose to have diverse viewpoints expressed, and readers will notice that this purpose was fully achieved in the discussion of the environment preserved in this book. We hope that what follows will clear up some confusion, encourage constructive thinking on both sides of the political divide, and help to raise the level of debate.

MICHAEL CROMARTIE

1

Managing the Planet: The Politics of 'The Environment'

Charles T. Rubin

If anyone were to suggest that in all discussion of politics and human society we would do well to confine ourselves to the intellectual horizons of Marxism, we would know immediately that we were dealing with an ideologue, and either pity his ignorance or despise his arrogance. But our sensitivity to "isms" is not equally well developed in all areas in which they arise. Consider the anxious efforts well-intentioned people will make to assure us that in their hearts they believe in environmentalism. George Bush wanted to be known not as a huntin' and fishin' president, not as a conservation president, not as a nature-loving president, but as an environmental president. People who believe that free and responsible human beings are best able to live in harmony with nature call themselves "free market environmentalists." A great many of those relatively few and hardy souls who criticize the "environmental movement" for one reason or another do so having asserted that, whatever the weight of their criticisms, they still consider themselves "environmentalists."

"Environmentalism" so pervades our outlook that we do not see it

Charles T. Rubin is associate professor of political science at Duquesne University, Pittsburgh. He is the author of *The Green Crusade: Rethinking the Roots of Environmentalism* (The Free Press, 1994).

as an ideology, a particular set of beliefs. To cast it as such is likely to produce vociferous objection, on at least two grounds. On the one hand, environmentalism will be said to be, not an ideology, but the most lucid common sense about the need to improve our relationship to the world around us. On the other hand, its defenders may say that "environmentalism" is a catch-all phrase for so many different points of view that it hardly achieves the internal coherence we associate even with loose use of the word "ideology," and bears no likeness whatsoever to a formal ideology like Marxism.

William Ruckelshaus, two-time administrator of the Environmental Protection Agency, has summed up the first objection: "Most people do not need a scientific panel to tell them that air is not supposed to be brown, that streams are not supposed to ignite and stink, that beaches are not supposed to be covered with raw sewage."[1] But this argument suggests a deeper issue. There is no immaculate perception of environmental problems, any more than there is of any other public-policy area. For generations, what we now call substandard sanitation was simply considered a fact of life. It did not become a "problem" until people began to think that something else was both possible and desirable. "Problems" come to exist when people can imagine that the world does not have to be the way it is, i.e., when they have a vision of the future that is different from the past, and when they think they possess the power to bring the vision to life.[2] Visions of this sort, of course, are such stuff as ideologies are made on.

This brings us to the second objection, concerning the diversity of environmental visions. Although there is certainly truth to this point, it is at best partial. Environmentalism is indeed riven by some serious disagreements among various schools of thought. Those who think that population is *the* environmental problem look askance at those who blame technology; those who focus on the problems that human beings create for themselves are criticized for a wrong-headed anthropocentrism by those who think we need to look first to the well-being of other forms of life; and so on.

But it did not stop us from speaking about "Marxism" to know that Stalinists were at knife's point with Trotskyites, or that Maoism was inconsistent with evolutionary socialism. These factions vied for the label of true Marxism; yet all were heirs to Marx. The existence of *some* kinds of diversity among environmentalists does not mean they have *no* common assumptions that make it reasonable to speak of them under a collective term. Indeed, when it is in their interest, such persons and groups happily use the collective label "environmentalists" themselves, to suggest the power of numbers that rests behind the ideal they are articulating. Only when they are on the defensive is the diversity card likely to be played.

Recall also that for most of the history of thinking about man and nature, people had no recourse to the rubrics "environment," "environmental," and "environmentalist." These words, as we use them today, are very recent additions to our language, which strongly suggests there was something distinctive that we needed to describe with them. Usually we don't get new words—particularly new words that proceed to establish themselves as tenaciously as these have done—unless we need them.

If there are indeed common assumptions that are definitive of environmentalism, what are they? In my book *The Green Crusade: Rethinking the Roots of Environmentalism,* I delve into the core ideas of environmentalism through a look at the popularizers who have defined this new "common sense" for us, authors like Rachel Carson, Barry Commoner, Paul Ehrlich, and E. F. Schumacher.[3] From close examination of these writers' arguments I argue that environmentalism is generally defined by a concern for man's relationship to nature that arises out of utopian and totalitarian political programs for the complete reformation of human life on earth.

Even before I explain what I mean by "utopian and totalitarian," let me hasten to add that not all environmentalists fall into these two categories. Certainly, for example, free-market environmentalists or anarcho-environmentalists are not totalitarians. But we may still raise the question: Is their understanding of what makes a given situation an "environmental problem" informed by the utopian or totalitarian framework that is established by "environmentalism"? The question is of more than academic interest. If those who eschew totalitarianism accept the "environmental problem" mindset, then the means they suggest to solve or ameliorate those problems are almost certainly going to appear inadequate or half-hearted, hence casting doubt on their environmental credentials. If, on the other hand, they do not accept the "problem" definitions proposed by environmentalism, then what is to be gained by adopting a rubric that, as we will see, has the most problematic consequences?

In *The Green Crusade* I suggest that environmentalism is utopian in the sense that the project it puts forward contains such tensions or internal contradictions that the goals sought either will never be achieved or, if achieved, will have harmful consequences. In this essay, I will focus not on this utopianism but rather on the totalitarian aspect of environmentalism.

The Environmental Whole

What, exactly, is "the environment"? Some thirty years of environmental concern have produced less precision on this question than one might expect. Not all basic texts in "environmental science" even bother to define the term.[4] When definitions are given, they do not always agree on what is included or excluded. Start with the modest notion of *an* environment, the physical and biotic factors that define a given organism's world. These worlds overlap; I am part of the chipmunk's environment and the chipmunk is part of mine. Environments are thus interconnected. From that observation it is but a short (even if scientifically highly dubious) step to Barry Commoner's "law of ecology" that "everything is connected to everything else."[5] If that is so, *an* environment becomes *the* environment.

But words, carefully used, should give us the means of discriminating between this and that. If everything is connected to everything else, what is *not* part of the environment? Paul Ehrlich, stung by accusations that environmentalism is elitist, concluded that "slums, cockroaches, and rats are ecological problems, too. The correction of ghetto conditions in Detroit is neither more nor less important than saving the Great Lakes—both are imperative."[6] Likewise, the 1970 National Environmental Policy Act (NEPA) placed "safe, healthful, productive, and aesthetically and culturally pleasing surroundings" and "diversity and variety of individual choice" under the environmental rubric.[7] In *Metropolitan Edison Co. v. People Against Nuclear Energy* (460 U.S. 766), Chief Justice Rehnquist rightly noted that almost any action of government could be reviewed under the NEPA environmental-impact provisions. His own narrower interpretation of the statute, as if it speaks only to "the physical environment—the world around us, so to speak," while quite broad enough, seems more an exercise by a restraining judiciary than of judicial restraint.[8]

Even with the above extensions of "the environment," we have still not reached its limit. The cutting edge of environmental wisdom now extends to outer space; some worry about earth orbit pollution, space colonies, and possible human "impacts," admittedly remote, on extraterrestrial life.[9] It is no mere joke when a text in environmental law quotes comedian Peter Cook to the effect that the environment "embraces 'the universe and all that surrounds it.'"[10] No wonder there are now more environmental lawyers than labor lawyers.

And outer space is not the final frontier. Lynton Keith Caldwell, one of the architects of the National Environmental Policy Act, writes: "The environmental crisis is an outward manifestation of a crisis of the mind and spirit. There could be no greater misconception of its meaning than to believe it to be concerned only with endangered wildlife, human-made ugliness, and pollution."[11] Calls for spiritual renewal are welcome, but, as we will shall see, when they are driven by "environmental" necessity, they take on a distinctly problematic cast.

The Relation of the Parts

Another characteristic of "the environment," in addition to its all-inclusiveness, is that its parts are related to one another in a certain way. Here we find the lesson of a fragile web of life, widely popularized by Rachel Carson in *Silent Spring.* Carson's account of that connection was far more equivocal than it is usually portrayed to be. Sometimes the web was pictured as static and easily damaged, sometimes as dynamic and readily capable of recovery. Sometimes the connections were portrayed as causing damage to be amplified in space and over time, sometimes as having a dampening effect. We may not be much more clear today about just when and where the environment is fragile, but the sense of a whole whose parts are delicately bound together is usually taken as a given. That assumption makes it possible to attach global importance to *any* event. An article on the decline in the number of amphibians noticed in various places throughout the world quotes biologist Marc Hayes as saying that it is "clearly a global problem—some kind of climate effect," and speaks of "interrelated trends" like global warming and ozone loss, even though it also offers a number of local, non-climate-based possible explanations for the decline.[12]

A troublesome situation need not share in a unified global explanation in order to be a genuine cause for concern. To understand high infant mortality, for example, we apply a number of plausible explanations depending on the local circumstances observed; we do not believe that there must be one common, world-wide cause in order for the problem to be taken seriously. But conceptualizing situations under the rubric of "the environment" promotes a tendency to find a single or global cause.

That cause is almost certainly going to be something human beings have done, given the assumptions that go into "the environment." Left alone, the fragile web of life is assumed to be capable of taking care of itself. In nature, we are told, the parts fit together splendidly; nature poses no problems to itself that it cannot handle. But human beings can disrupt natural balances with a speed or an intensity or a scope that nature cannot accommodate. Never mind that there is increasingly a sense among ecologists that speaking of nature in terms of balance or even homeostasis is extremely misleading. We will continue to be alerted to more human behaviors that require control, as the environmentalists uncover ever more subtle threats to the integrity of "the environment."

Therefore, environmental activists and popularizers are rife with global schemes of economic and political control, whether in the name of safer technology, a "no-growth" society, or radical population reduction. Because they must deal with the total environment, with everything, because everything is connected to everything else, because we can never do something that has only local effects, these schemes of reform and rejuvenation often take on a totalitarian character.

I do not use that word lightly. Nor do I mean to suggest by it that all greens are just reds or black-shirts in disguise (although some are), or that all environmentalists want to replicate the horrors of twentieth-century tyrants but "in a good cause" (although some might). Yet I believe the charge is justified, and in a rather precise sense. In his fine book *In Defense of People,* Richard John Neuhaus suggests a reasonable way of formulating the basis for viewing environmentalism as totalitarian:

> . . . [A]s much as we may credit the humane sensitivities and democratic convictions of its authors, the totalitarian bias of much ecological literature is inescapable. The essential idea that society should be reorganized around a "single guiding concept" reveals a

totalist approach to social structure. All demurrers to the contrary, this assumption is the cornerstone of ideological opposition to the pluralism that most Americans who have thought about the matter claim to cherish. The call for an embracing "coherence" that can overcome chaotically threatening fragmentation has marked all integralist and authoritarian political movements. . . .

[T]he demand for social coherence suggests an ideological rigidity and political centralism that is, I believe, foreign to the American social experiment at its best. . . . When the call for coherence is joined to the single guiding concept of survival, the implications are particularly grave.[13]

Totalitarianism brings all things into coherence. As Lynton Caldwell suggested, the totalizing perspective of "the environment" necessarily extends to sweeping revision of ethical beliefs and "value structures." Biblical religion—monotheism itself—is particularly suspect. Historian Lynn White's initial foray into this topic, blaming certain aspects of the Judeo-Christian tradition for the environmental crisis, appeared in the magazine *Science;* for many environmentalists, skepticism about religion is part and parcel of their scientific creed. But White's analysis is positively friendly compared with some of what has followed. As many "Deep Ecologists" tell the story, the pagan world had a proper reverence for natural things, setting up temples on mountains, in caves, and at streams and springs. The victory of Christianity meant the destruction of such places; they became sites of fear and loathing, abodes of the Evil One.[14] Or again, Garrett Hardin, having made species survival very close to the highest value, finds it necessary to reject "Thou shalt not kill" in favor of "Thou shalt not suffer carrying capacity to be exceeded."[15]

We need not turn to such a hard-boiled skeptic as Hardin, or to people who might have pantheistic proclivities to begin with, to see this logic at work. The premise of Father Thomas Berry's *The Dream of the Earth* is that modern, Western thought is turning Earth into a "wasteworld."[16] Christianity, with its view of the world as a "one-time emerging process," closed off the pagan cyclical vision and thus opened the door to the modern scientific and technological progress that is destroying the Earth.[17] Furthermore, Christianity's reliance on "extrinsic spiritual interpretations," by which I take it that Berry means God, means that it "objectified" human creativity, and thus failed to see what we do as simply another expression of the emerging and enduring power of nature.[18] Even science and technology could be salvaged if we recognized them as the myth-making of our time; but it is perhaps safer to hearken to the "primal people of the world . . . [who] call the entire civilized world back to a more authentic mode of being," for in these cultures the revelatory power of nature is celebrated, and human beings thus live in a harmony with nature that is impossible for us.[19] "Within this context the human community was energized by the cosmic rituals wherein ultimate meaning was attained, absolute mysteries were enacted, human needs were fulfilled. . . . These ancient ritual patterns and the personal spiritual disciplines were sufficient to keep the great societies within their proper energy cycles."[20]

Leery of seeming to idealize our ability to live in harmony with nature, Berry presses us to accept the more authentic mode of existence he advocates "with all the severity of its demands."[21] It is unfortunate, and conducive to just the romanticism he claims to reject, that Berry does not elaborate on what these severe demands are. But we might get a hint in some things he says about the United States. While we pride ourselves, Berry notes, on our "sense of political and social transformation that would release us from age-old tyrannies," he believes that the *actual* result of the American experiment has been a "savage assault" on the order of nature of just the sort that he claims the age-old tyrannies did not perpetrate.[22] Indeed, some of the age-old tyrannies are just the sorts of places where the essential, revelatory human experiences we are blocked from were able to occur. Those who came to this country, Berry notes, thought of themselves as escaping Egypt and reaching the promised land.[23] Evidently Berry prefers Egypt.

Planet Management

More mainstream environmentalists may cringe at such excesses, but the same tendencies creep into their own thinking. Once upon a time, it was only a counterculture publication like the *Whole Earth Catalog* that would teach, "We are as gods and might as well get good at it." Now, an establishment journal like *Scientific American* can publish a collection of essays under the title *Managing Planet Earth.*[24] The goal of such management is "sustainable development." This remarkably slippery concept seems to add to conventional ideas of development the goal of a harmonious and unified managerial capacity, to ensure that (as the U.N.'s Brundtland Report put it) "exploitation of resources, the direction of investments, the orientation of technological development, and institutional change" meet "human needs and aspirations."[25] We are thus to achieve globally skills that would be the envy of anyone who has ever tried to run a five-person office, let alone a large corporation.

Such visions make the best the enemy of the better, creating dissatisfaction with everything we have achieved or indeed could possibly achieve. When Friends of the Earth wanted to fault the Rio Summit, they pointed out its "failure to set a new direction for life on earth."[26] This remark represents analysis serious enough to quote on the front page of the *New York Times*—a sign either of the pervasive effect of green totalitarianism on our thought or of the falling standards of America's newspaper of record.

Total control would require total information. The green totalitarians require complete information not only about resources, investments, and technology but also about the ecology of every species of living thing. Witness E. O. Wilson's plan for a comprehensive catalog of all species of life on earth.[27] Here surely is an effort whose ambitious scope is beyond even that of the much vaunted Human Genome Project, if only because genes do not try to hide from us. But the environmental perspective so pervades our thinking that it can be seen as controversial only from the point of view of the most narrow self-interest, as if the question "What happens if some rare species shows up on my land?" were the only one that could be asked. Wilson's own notion that such a list is required in order that we not overlook some benefit that nature can have for us is merely reversed by Deep Ecology's aspiration to create a world in which human purposes would be simply one among all the other needs of life and non-life on the planet. In short, nobody wonders seriously about what we would do with the list once we had it.

But what to do with complete information is, for the present, the least of our worries. We see the price of attempting comprehensive regulation in the face of incomplete information in the many environmental horror stories that never prove to be true. We are not, as Paul Ehrlich would have expected, subject to food rationing in the United States today.[28] Love Canal is now being resettled, not only because of improved monitoring and containment, but because it took years for the furor to die down enough that people could actually pay attention to the evidence, which was that there was little or no reason to suspect a health threat. The man largely responsible for the evacuation of Times Beach suggests in retrospect that he probably made a mistake.[29] Congress rushes to legislate extensive pollution control on sulphur dioxide in order to stop acid rain, while the largest-scale study of the problem ever undertaken suggests it is not, in fact, much of a problem. The Superfund program combines inadequate understanding of the character of the toxic-waste problem with unrealistically high expectations for what can be done about it; with that kind of start, why should we be surprised when billions of dollars are spent to so minimal an effect?

Why in the face of these experiences we should have faith in global management may appear as a mystery. But here again it has to do with the constraints we impose on our thinking when we start with "the environment." For such "local" regulatory problems are arguably tied to our failure to take a big enough view, to appreciate fully what it means that "everything is connected to everything else." We are, it might be argued, failing to be comprehensive *enough* in our outlook, and hence we are paying attention to the wrong sort of problem in the first place.

Gore's Global Vision

This argument is at the core of Al Gore's *Earth in the Balance: Ecology and the Human Spirit.* He is at pains to get us to pay more attention to global, "strategic" threats—issues like climate change and ozone destruction—because if these problems are not solved, cleaning up all the toxic sites in the world will not save us.[30] Proper attention to such threats requires not just complete spiritual renewal (whether a man who morally equates *Kristallnacht* with environmental damage is a reliable guide in this area seems dubious) but also a global Marshall Plan to remake the world's economy and technology.[31] Gore says, no doubt sincerely, that he is against world government and totalitarianism, but the problem he sets out and the solution he outlines do not make this demurral a mere formality.[32] He wants a world acting as cohesively to fight environmental threats as the Allies fought the Nazis or as the West opposed Communism.[33]

Leaving aside the possibility that Gore overstates the actual degree of cohesion in these instances, we might well wonder whether the exceptional circumstances that go along with total war are such as to conduce to political moderation of any sort. No less an authority on this matter than Churchill noted that in peacetime, many a problem "solves itself or sinks to an altogether lower range if time, patience and phlegm are used."[34] Yet Gore wants to convince his readers that we stand at the kind of extremity that should make Churchill's suggestion seem as misplaced as if it were made in the midst of desperate conflict.

A global threat requires the rejection of politics as usual, and it is no surprise that the cover of Gore's best-selling book features the most powerful icon of environmentalism: a photograph of our planet taken from outer space. The world, we are often told, is small within this vastness. Seeing it whole, we can even believe that it could be managed as a whole. That view is promoted most of all by the non-appearance of things human. For even though environmentalists love to liken humanity to terrestrial cancer, in the view from outer space human achievements do not appear even as a rash on the body of the earth goddess Gaia. National boundaries and all they imply about human freedom and despotism, the problems of governance and conflicting principles of governance, are invisible. Indeed, everything that touches us on a daily basis—the world we really live in—is missing. Appropriately to a view from outer space, the "whole earth" image is an alien vision.

The Problem of Human Nature

Yet this image precisely reflects the lessons that "the environment" instills in its failure to appreciate the human element. What happens when people perversely insist on clinging to the old ways, to their environmentally incorrect belief systems? What if the "human aspirations" that sustainable development is supposed to satisfy risk the extinction of the spotted owl? As soon as we ask such questions, we realize the extent to which human nature is going to be as much of a problem from the perspective of green totalitarianism as it was for the red variety.

Red totalitarianism "solved" the problem of human nature with the Gulag. Some greens have thought up a different use for barbed wire. So mainstream a foundation as the Pew Charitable Trusts is funding research into how vast settled tracts of the United States could be returned to wilderness.[35] Communities, traditions, history are not just *subordinated* to the whole-earth perspective—they are invisible to it.

Should the mere resettlement of human beings prove insufficient, we can always work for their elimination, just as a cancer must be excised or a proliferating bacterium stopped. It may be only a few among a fringe group like Earth First! who ever seriously hoped that the AIDS virus would greatly reduce human numbers, whatever their newsletter might have suggested.[36] Such outspoken misanthropy is relatively rare among environmentalists. But covert misanthropy is not far from the surface; the fact that we do not see it for what it is is once again excused only by the framework we have adopted. There are, for example, the stirring words that introduce Paul Ehrlich's *The Population Bomb,* describing how he first felt the emotional impact of the population problem in a Delhi slum:

> The streets seemed alive with people. People eating, people washing, people sleeping. People visiting, arguing, and screaming. People thrusting their hands through the taxi window, begging. People defecating and urinating. People clinging to buses. People herding animals. People, people, people, people. As we moved slowly through the mob, hand horn squawking, the dust, noise, heat, and cooking fires gave the scene a hellish aspect. Would we ever get to our hotel? All three of us were, frankly, frightened.[37]

We do not have to believe that a Delhi slum is the high point of human existence to wonder just what Ehrlich saw that seemed to him so far outside the realm of normal human behavior as to deserve to be called "hellish."

Becoming Like Sasquatch

Even when environmentalists manage to restrain their dislike of people as people, a suspicion of present-day human culture and indeed of reason itself is taking hold (a phenomenon not confined to environmental circles). Some Deep Ecologists, tacitly accepting the proposition that man is the animal with *logos*, go beyond their nostalgia for "primal cultures" to an aspiration to create a new version of man that eliminates this problematic trait. The model, as urged by the sociologist William Devall, is to be Sasquatch, the mythical humanoid of the Northwest, who lives comfortably in his forest home, without need of artifice or intelligence:

> Perhaps Sasquatch represents a more mature kind of human, a future primal being. . . . While we, who are children of technocratic civilization, must bring cumbersome technology into the forest to provide shelter and to satisfy our other needs and desires, Sasquatch dwells freely in the forest unencumbered by the burden of complex and complicated technology.
>
> While we are torn with desire for more power over other people and domination over nature, Sasquatch dwells peacefully and unobtrusively with other creatures of the forest. While we are dependent on huge bureaucracies such as schools, governments and military agencies, Sasquatch is independent and autonomous and fully integrated with the forest.[38]

Some see not totalitarianism but anarchism in such expressions of Deep Ecology; after all, Devall even takes a bold stand against schools. But totalitarians always promise "genuine" freedom, i.e., the creation of a context in which human beings can live in accord with the highest necessities. Thus, to suggest, as Devall does, that the genuine exercise of independence and autonomy requires a being who does not yet exist, is to promise total control of human beings as we know them.

Another vision of the future, apparently growing in popularity, is equally consistent with the fear that humanity, if left to its own devices, will pretty well screw things up. This is a fear that arises reasonably enough when the human task is made out to be global management. In *Scientific American,* Marvin Minsky, a pioneer in artificial intelligence, has suggested that tough questions like "How many people should occupy the earth? What sorts of people should they be? How should we share the available space?" would be more readily answered if we could design our descendants.[39] By this he has in mind, following the argument of another artificial-intelligence proponent (Hans Moravec), the supposed evolutionary necessity that robots will displace human beings. The thought that we are preparing the way for a "postbiological" or "supernatural" world is just the other side of the coin on which Sasquatch appears.[40] Nothing will so grace our presence on the environmental stage as our departure from it.

Whatever plausibility such aspirations have depends on a view of our situation in relation to the world around us that is decisively informed by, although perhaps not entirely due to, the hopes and fears that are created when we conceptualize that relationship in terms of "the environment." In part, I admit, what we see here is a result of working through some of the basic premises of modernity, with its emphasis on the control of nature for human purposes. So profound an exponent of modernity as Francis Bacon seemed to understand that this might well mean control of human nature as well. There is some irony that modernity should, as it were, lose its nerve on this point and thus have recourse to the hope that evolution of one kind or another will solve our problem for us. But in any case, we go well beyond such "classic" expositions of the modern project when we seek global security equally for all forms of life, which is the "hyper-modern" project that environmentalism puts before us.

Between the Extremes

Between the extremes of managing planet earth and animalizing or mechanizing humanity lies a fundamentally different approach that rejects the totalizing perspective of "the environment" and instead addresses problems singly, as they emerge, close to home. Rene Dubos was a major contributor to environmental globalism in its earliest stages, but to his credit he came to have second thoughts. This included a rethinking of the usefulness of the term "environment":

> The word *environment* does not convey the quality of the relationships that humankind can ideally establish with the Earth. Its widespread use points in fact to the present poverty of those relationships. In common parlance, as well as etymologically, the environment consists of things around us, out there, that act on us and on which we act. Whether good or bad, the physical components of our surroundings are foreign to us and we are foreign to them.
>
> We expect more of the environment in which we live, however, than conditions suitable for our health, resources to run the economic machine, and whatever is meant by good ecological conditions. We want to experience the sensory, emotional, and spiritual satisfactions that can be obtained only from an intimate interplay, indeed from an identification with the places in which we live. This interplay and identification generate the spirit of place. The en-

vironment acquires the attributes of *place* through the fusion of the natural and the human order. All human beings have approximately the same fundamental needs for biologic and economic welfare, but the many different expressions of humanness can be satisfied only in particular places.[41]

The implications of thinking along the lines Dubos suggests here are profound, and he began to see many of them himself. This new awareness made him him less than popular on American campuses. "Faculty as well as students were surprised and somewhat annoyed," he wrote, "when I suggested that, instead of being exclusively concerned with the nation or the world as a whole, they should first consider more local situations." Among these latter Dubos had in mind not only the condition of fields and streams but "the messiness of public rooms on their campus and the disorder of their social relationships."[42]

Such prosaic aspects of our lives are hardly worth mentioning from the perspective of "the environment"; yet they are essential to the quality of life as we live it day by day. From the perspective of *place* we come to understand that our relationship to the world around us is not something special that requires new environmental ethics or philosophies, but is just part of the ongoing quest to be decent human beings. We will have to give up our aspirations to "save the earth" or "plan it for the planet." But we will find that a myriad of problems we can identify in our relationship to that part of nature that is well known and close to us can be addressed by individual efforts or voluntary associations. In fact, a good deal of grassroots activity is of this kind already. If we see how important it is to maintain the freedom to clean up our own backyards, then we will be less likely to think we are just doing our part to achieve some vision of a global utopia. Focusing on the particular, the local, and the possible will conduce to a shared sense of individual responsibility, and not to the evasions that result when we define problems in such comprehensive terms that only a powerful, centralized government can even begin to deal with them.

In conclusion, we would do little conceptual violence to "environmentalism" if we simply replaced the word "environment" with the word "everything," and likewise spoke of "everythingists" and "everythingism."[43] To do so would be to clarify why we show no satisfaction with those improvements in our relationship to nature that have been achieved, and, similarly, why we are always willing to raise the bar yet again. Contrary to its overt intention, "everythingism" does not finally teach us about limits, or moderation, or the need to acknowledge a power in the world greater than our own. Instead, like Hawthorne's Aylmer in "The Birthmark," it is in revolt against human imperfection and a world we do not fully understand. It only remains to be seen whether, like that deluded man of science, everythingism will destroy the object it ostensibly loves.

A Response

Andrew Kimbrell

When I was first asked to respond to Charles Rubin's generally negative conclusions about the environmental movement, I thought there might be little substantial disagreement between us. My criticisms of the movement are many, especially as regards the continuing reliance of environmentalists on obscure scientific debate rather than spiritual principles (including reflection on the sacred and sacramental aspects of nature, and our duty of stewardship). In addition, as a long-time attorney, writer, and activist in this area I have been continuously frustrated with how few environmentalists have made a larger critique of the dysfunctional philosophies and modes of production of modernity, of which the destruction of nature, however urgent a problem, is but a symptom.

However, after hearing Rubin's paper and reading his book, *The Green Crusade,* I have discovered that we strongly disagree about both the roots and the problems of environmentalism. As amply demonstrated by his presentation, Rubin has read all the right books. But he has read them for all the wrong reasons and has failed to understand their real message.

Before taking on the substance of Rubin's remarks I would like to comment on their tone. An unseemly snideness marks much of the current criticism of environmentalism, especially from the right. This

---

Andrew Kimbrell is the director of the International Center for Technology Assessment, in Washington, D.C. He is the author of *The Human Body Shop: The Engineering and Marketing of Life* (HarperCollins, 1993) and general editor of *The Green Lifestyle Handbook* (Holt, 1990).

snideness often finds its way into Rubin's work. For example, his book contains an inaccurate and grossly inadequate summary of the work of E. F. Schumacher, whom he calls a utopian and a totalitarian. Rubin ends his attack on Schumacher with the remark that for Schumacher "the accumulated wisdom of the East and West really culminates in an electric wheelbarrow."[1] This ill-tempered caricature falls apart if one actually reads Schumacher—for instance, the wonderful collection published under the title *Good Work*.[2] In the critical essay "Toward a Human Scale Technology" Schumacher openly announces that his analysis of technology and the environmental crisis is made "in the light of the gospel."[3] (He was, after all, a Catholic convert.) This remarkable essay is devoid of any environmental totalitarianism and utopianism. To the contrary, Shumacher is saying that the market system created its own kind of utopian idea, a consumer's heaven on earth governed by the "invisible hand" of commerce and the increasing totalitarian power of technology over people and nature.

The question Schumacher constantly addresses is, What kind of society gives all of us, as reasonable men and women, more of a chance to escape evil and achieve eternal salvation? He believes, quite sensibly, that our current market-and-technology-driven society is not a desirable one under this spiritual test, and that a new society based on appropriate technology and stewardship will offer less occasion for sin.

The Secular Trinity

Rubin's misrepresentation of Schumacher is part of his ambitious attempt to convince us that there is a new totalitarian specter haunting our society, an emerging environmental dictatorship based in a fanatic utopian zeal. He suggests that this new "green" menace is replacing the old "red" menace as the central threat to our freedom and democracy. But despite his best efforts, Rubin does not convince us that this environmental monster, this "Greenenstein" that Rubin created from equal parts of creation spirituality, ecological science, and New Age humbuggery, exists.

Moreover, in the current political climate, Rubin's alarmist warnings about environmental totalitarianism take on a touch of the absurd. During the 1960s and 1970s—when many of us were working on the National Environmental Policy Act, the Clean Water Act, the Clean

Air Act, and other similar legislation—there was much optimism about the environmental movement. Over the last fifteen years, however, little important environmental legislation has been passed. Clinton's first two years in office saw no such legislation passed, and now the new Republican majority in Congress is proposing to roll back most of the environmental laws that have been in place for over two decades. So much for "Greenenstein" cowing the public and dictating national policy.

I suspect, however, that the real problem Rubin and others have with environmentalism—defined as the growing concern about the destruction of nature and our failure to steward the creation—has little to do with any real fears about green totalitarianism or utopianism becoming the new communism. Rather, these concerns are simply code words to hide their real objection, which is that environmentalism is a heresy to their belief system.

While it is little mentioned in discussions of this sort, modernity has a dogmatic belief system, one apparently fully shared by Rubin. This secular religion even has its own trinity, which is as central to the religion of modernity as the sacred trinity is to Christianity. What is this new trinity? (1) Science will ultimately allow us to know everything. (2) Technology will allow us to do everything. (3) The market will allow us to buy everything. This, not any notion of nature, is the real utopianism of modern capitalist culture and has been for generations. Since the deeper environmental thinkers question the hegemony of science, technology, and the market, they are heretics, and the new secular inquisitors like Rubin set out to discredit them, lest their heresies actually undermine the new religion.

An examination of the tragic results of our blind faith in science, technology, and the market will bring us far closer to understanding the roots of environmentalism and the need for environmental regulations than Rubin's analysis. At the outset, Rubin has specifically eshewed any historical understanding of the roots of environmentalism and has instead opted for the view that the environmental movement was created by several important authors of the 1960s and 1970s (Carson, Commoner, Ehrlich, Schumacher).[4] While Rubin's "book review" approach gives him ample opportunity for *ad hominem* attacks on prominent recent environmental thinkers, it does little to advance our understanding of environmentalism.

Environmentalism was actually born, not in the 1960s, but rather as part of the conservation movement. The call for conservation was a key element in the progressive era of reform, which reached its peak at the beginning of the twentieth century. At that time scientists, technicians, and managers began to see that unbridled capitalism was not sustainable. For one thing, it was destroying the very resource base on which production depended. It was also making cities unlivable and spawning massive social unrest. The aim of the conservation movement was therefore to make more efficient use of natural resources than was occurring under unregulated capitalism. In his important book *Conservation and the Gospel of Efficiency,* Samuel P. Hays ably describes how the progressive reformers' attempt to manage resources was simply part of a larger managerial revolution that included plans to manage immigration, population, education, labor, and virtually every other aspect of society.[5]

Fictitious Commodities

The managerial revolution started by the progressive reformers over a century ago has caused much of the unfortunate bureaucratic technocracy that is apparent not only in current environmental regulation but throughout our society. However, while it is easy to find fault with the progressive solution, it is important to remember that the progressives were addressing very real problems created by the market system. For, while the market system began to produce unprecedented wealth in industrial societies, it also had at its core a contradiction that at any moment threatened the viability of the entire system.

Unlike past societies, modern society based on the market system treats virtually everything as a commodity, as something produced for sale. However, not everything is a commodity. Most importantly, both labor and land are fictitious commodities, since they are either not produced at all (land) or not for sale (labor). Yet early on, the fiction that land and labor were commodities was very effective in perpetuating the market system. The market created a market price for labor, called wages, and a market price for land, called rent. But labor is just another name for man, and land is just another name for nature. As noted by economist Karl Polanyi, "the commodity fiction handed over the fate of man and nature to the play of an automaton [the free market] running on its own grooves and governed by its own laws."[6]

Treating non-commodities as commodities exacts a high price. If labor is divorced from the person and seen simply as a commodity, then anybody's energy is for sale. In early capitalism, child labor became common, and workers toiled under horrific conditions for wages that could not provide a livelihood. The rebellion of workers against being treated as mere commodities began to threaten the stability of the entire society.

By the early twentieth century, numerous reformers were attempting to mitigate the effects of treating labor as a commodity. Under growing public pressure, government bureaucracies were formed to deal with the labor problem (the Department of Labor was set up in 1917). Soon legislation was passed protecting working children, reducing work hours, mandating safer work places, establishing minimum wages, and so on. Even today, of course, a huge bureaucracy continues to defend society from the total disruption that would result if labor were treated wholly as a commodity.

The same scenario happened with land, and this is the real root of the environmental movement. Land, though it is not a commodity, was treated as such throughout the nineteenth century in the United States. By the turn of the twentieth century, Gifford Pinchot and other conservationists began to realize that the uncontrolled sale and use of land was destroying the natural resource base, and thus the production base, at an alarming rate. So they began to put into place various bureaucracies and protections to try to keep land from being treated solely as a commodity. As production technologies increased and the use of fossil fuels and pesticides increased, more and more regulation was needed. Now, since the market has gone global, the managers are attempting to globalize measures that lead to the most efficient use of natural resources.

So while we can all share in Rubin's frustration over the massive bureaucracies that control so much of our lives, including the increasingly global bureaucracies that involve environmental regulation, let us at least identify the true culprit. It is near ludicrous to assert that the massive technocracies of our time are the fault of the Rachel Carsons and E. F. Schumachers. The fault really lies in the very market ideology that Rubin and others so revere. There's a continuing irony in the constant complaints of free-market adherents about bureaucracy and regulation, since it is the very treatment of non-commodities as commodities—an essential component of the market system—that has caused these technocracies to grow and flourish.

They are inevitable in a society that treats land and labor as commodities, and where social relationships are based not on kinship, religion, or community but on markets and contracts.

Thus if Rubin really wanted to discover the roots of environmentalism, he would have done better to start with Adam Smith and his successors. For it was their triumph that inevitably led to massive government interference with the use of resources, in order to protect those resources from total commodification.

Technological Totalitarianism

As an alternative to much of our current environmental policy (and contrary to the progressivist solution) Rubin advocates an end to national and international environmental regulation and instead calls on us to "clean up our backyards." Given the current globalization of the market economy and its growing usurpation of national and local governance (as reflected in international trade agreements such as GATT), Rubin's call for local action seems naïve. It is not just the market but also current technology that works to make local action generally ineffective. For our current technological milieu is in itself totalitarian. Had Rubin read his Schumacher more sympathetically, he perhaps would have understood that technological totalitarianism, not any purported environmental utopianism, is the true totalitarianism of our time.

Technology is never neutral. It always represents power over something or someone. The question is always whether the power is appropriate. Seen from this perspective, technology is legislation. The technologies we develop will affect the political structure of our society. We cannot live in a democratic society if our society is built around totalitarian technologies, that is, technologies that we cannot take real responsibility for and that cannot be truly responsive to us. Technologies that we *can* be responsible for and that *are* responsive to us are democratic technologies.

Let's look at one example of how technology legislates the structure of society. For decades one of the fiercest conservative versus liberal, free-market versus environmentalist arguments has been over nuclear power. Conservatives who profess to be against government regulation, and for community control and individual autonomy, nevertheless adamantly support nuclear power. To see the incongruity of these positions, consider what is needed for a nuclear power plant: a massive capital investment well beyond the means of a community; a military elite, because nuclear materials can be used for military weapons and must be strictly controlled; a scientific elite to build and operate the nuclear power plant; large bureaucracies to ensure the safety of these highly dangerous power sources, to manage energy distribution (nuclear plants produce massive amounts of energy that is to be sold and disseminated over a large area), and to dispose of radioactive waste, which can have over a 100,000-year half-life.

Conservatives who support nuclear power may profess their devotion to democracy and local control as well as their opposition to bureaucracy; but as long as they support totalitarian technologies like nuclear power, they will inevitably get a society that requires huge capital accumulations, a military elite, a scientific elite, huge and complex bureaucracies, and centralized ownership and control of resources. Solar power, by contrast, actually embodies many of the political aims of conservatives. Solar power does not require a huge capital investment, or scientific and military elites, or large bureaucracies. It can be controlled locally or individually. It is democratic.

Clearly, if you build the body of your society with totalitarian technologies and technocracies (i.e., nuclear power, factory farms, centralized media, massive corporations, huge government bureaucracies) rather than democratic ones, you will have a totalitarian society, regardless of its stated political system. And predictably you become, as most U.S. citizens have become, virtually powerless inside that technological grid. You cannot control the job you have, when and if you will become unemployed, the quality of the food you eat or the water you drink, what is in the air you breathe, what is taught to your children, how your tax dollars are spent, and so on.

The problem of totalitarian technology becomes a really central problem for acting and thinking locally. Living lives on a community basis where we truly have control over our "backyards" will be an impossibility unless we restructure our society, not to create utopia, but simply to free ourselves from the institutional evils endemic to totalitarian technology. We need to construct our society around human-scale, democratic technologies. We will, of course, abuse even these technologies, for we are fallen creatures; but at least we will have the ability, which we currently do not have, to be responsible for what we do and to have our technologies responsive to us.

Restructuring our society's technological base is obviously a huge undertaking. One of the problems of the environmental movement, in my opinion, is its virtual ignoring of this issue. Because it has had a relationship with the left, environmentalism has emphasized the politics of the means of production. Its focus has tended to be on a more even distribution and ownership of these means. What has been virtually forgotten for almost a century is the question of what politics, what theology, what vision of ourselves and nature inhere in the very technologies that we use. Until we analyze those questions, we're not going to come anywhere close to resolving our problems with nature, nor are we going to achieve something that Charles Rubin and the rest of us want, which is the freedom both to think locally and to act locally.

Comments

Peter Bakken: What would happen if we applied the basic logic of Charles Rubin's paper, not to the notion of environment, but to the notion of creation? Creation is likewise an all-inclusive concept. It also posits—in the Deuteronomic tradition in the Bible, the prophetic tradition, and so on—this connection between the human spirit and the condition of the world around us. Suppose we use "creation" rather than "everything" as the replacement term in Rubin's last paragraph; it would begin: "We would do little conceptual violence to 'environmentalism' if we simply replaced the word 'environmental' with the word 'creation' and likewise spoke of 'creationists' and 'creationism.'" I am reminded of Vine Deloria's book *God Is Red,* which appeared at about the same time as Richard Neuhaus's *In Defense of People.* He basically accuses the Christian tradition of having a totalizing perspective and argues for a polycentric, pluralistic approach to religion over against the single story of creation, single thread of salvation history.

Charles Rubin also mentions that we "show no satisfaction with those improvements in our relationship to nature that have been achieved, and similarly . . . are always willing to raise the bar yet again." What that called to my mind was the statement by St. Augustine, "O Lord, thou hast made us for thyself, and our hearts are restless until they find their rest in thee." It doesn't seem to me that the notion of environmentalism is really that misanthropic after all. One of the mainsprings of wanting to take a global perspective in certain senses is precisely this self-transcendence of the human spirit, which I think is what distinguishes us from the rest of creation and

---

Note: These participants are identified on pages 151-52.

enables us to talk about creation and to care about creation in ways that are not simply reducible to human preferences. It seems to me that what is really misanthropic is the Procrustean reading of human values and human ideals that reduces them to preferences, to matters of exchange and commodities—that makes us simply taxpayers or consumers or voters.

Charles Rubin: Is religion totalizing? Yes, but if we are talking about Judeo-Christian religion, it is totalizing—but with the understanding that human beings are flawed. Environmentalism doesn't tend to acknowledge that human beings are flawed, that it is part of us to be wrong or stupid or venal. From the perspective of mainstream environmentalism, nothing stands in the way of its utopian schemes; but religion says that something *does* stand in the way of our achieving, by our own efforts, the perfection of society.

Isn't *creation* also a broad term? Yes, but it isn't creation*ism,* while it *is* environmental*ism,* and that's a crucial difference. Barry Commoner and Garrett Hardin and Paul Ehrlich aren't interested in creation. Creation involves an entirely different moral universe from that which is occupied by much of mainstream environmentalism. I would be quite happy with people who wanted to say, Let's not talk about the environment, let's talk about creation. There's a moral richness as well as a moral ambiguity about that kind of discussion that I simply don't see in much environmental talk.

Fred Smith: I don't understand the antipathy to, the pejorative treatment of, the "commoditization" of nature. It seems to me that it's not only inevitable but happened ten thousand years ago, that man has already touched all parts of nature. The romantic idea of a world that knows not man is silly. Man is already there; the question is what kind of relationship man will have to nature. I would argue that things are valued only to the extent that we will sacrifice to protect them. Exchanges give the world value. Prices are one way we express these exchanges, but only one way. Many exchanges are not priced, are not in the market system.

For the last hundred years America has been imbued with two collectivist managerial visions: the Muir view that the world should be managed for preservation purposes, and the Pinchot view that the world should be managed for materialistic purposes. I believe both forms of the collectivist vision are obsolete. We've tried the idea that man knows enough to do everything. The idea that science knows everything, that technology can do everything, that "scientific management" resolves all problems, is over, I think. Hayek wrote a book called *The Fatal Conceit* arguing that mankind's genius over the last thousand years has been to create institutions that allow fallible humans to act more altruistically. We have moderated conflict, we have allowed value diversity, we have allowed freedom of choice, we have created wealth—all this gives people more opportunities to live their lives as they want to. We should focus more on the institutional framework.

"Ecological privatization" is a way of enriching our ability to relate meaningfully to nature. America cherishes the concept of separation of church and state, the idea that values can be so critical and yet so in conflict with one another that the resolution cannot be made politically or collectively but must be resolved privately. The cathedrals of God are built and financed by those individuals who believe, not by the taxpayer! We have separation of church and state. The eco-theocracy of today is demanding a special role, the role of a secular religion that all of us, whether we agree with the thesis or not, will have to submit our money to support. I think we ought to separate church and state in the ecology area as well as elsewhere. Ecological privatization allows us to address the hubris question; I think it is wrong to disparage such "commoditization" of nature.

Andrew Kimbrell: The original use of land solely as a commodity, particularly in the nineteenth century, caused all sorts of problems. If you buy up some forested mountain land and cut the forest down, then you've created various problems for the rivers at the bottom of those mountains and the farms along those rivers. So a large number of regulations and bureaucracies developed, in order to protect certain forests from being cut down, to zone certain property for one type of activity, and so on. It was simply a matter of protecting the resource base. That's what Gifford Pinchot was into: efficiency. Now if you were to treat your children *efficiently,* giving them the minimum food and minimum affection that can produce maximum good grades, you'd be considered pathological. We don't treat anything we truly care about primarily on an efficiency basis. What we have is an empathy-based versus an efficiency-based environmental movement.

Ron Sider: I agree with a number of Charles Rubin's criticisms of environmentalism. But I think he's guilty of tarring everyone with the same brush. It's rather like suggesting that all Protestant evangelicals are like Jim Bakker and all investment bankers are like Michael Milken. That's at least confusing if not dishonest, and it doesn't help us think carefully. Lots of orthodox Christians are deeply concerned with the environment and are neither utopian nor totalitarian.

Rubin asks, Why use the term *environment?* Because it's a useful term for talking about a particular set of concerns not identical with making the economy more just and productive, not identical with running family life properly, or with any other set of concerns. To suggest, as Rubin does, that there's no problem until people think so is a strange kind of subjectivism. If the water is bad, if it's making people ill, then that is an objective problem even if those suffering its effects don't think there's anything they can do about it and don't even realize that the water is a problem.

To criticize Al Gore by talking about a global Marshall Plan aims the criticism at the wrong point. If Gore exaggerates the problem and there's no need for some kind of global approach, then he is wrong. The issue is whether or not there is the kind of problem he talks about. I think it would have been rather stupid if, at the end of World War II, we decided to have each individual try to help Western Europe. We did need some kind of economic Marshall Plan.

One last point: Rubin seems to suggest that we have to choose between killing humans or killing spotted owls. Very seldom is that the choice. Usually the choice is between increased affluence or wiping out species. If I have to choose between humans dying or whole species of animals dying, I go with human beings. But that's seldom the choice in our affluent world.

Patrick Michaels: Andrew Kimbrell said that Greenenstein has had no power in the last fifteen years. But recall what has happened in those years—in fact, in the last five years. We have the Clean Air Act of 1990 with a price tag of $42 billion per year. We have the Rio Climate Treaty signed in 1992, a document that can be self-corrected and made binding upon our country apparently without the additional consent of the U.S. Senate. We have Agenda 21, with a price tag of $600 billion per year. It is "non-binding"; however, when I called a State Department office, I was told they viewed it as a "blueprint" and were doing their darndest to implement it. We have an exponential increase in regulatory power over the last five to ten years. This increase empowers generally at the expense of local sovereignty. And in things like Agenda 21, nations seem to be asked to surrender their sovereignty and also pay the price for their own suicide. I don't think that Greenenstein has been unsuccessful at all; I think he's growing rather rapidly.

Andrew Kimbrell: If I paid you, over five years, $3 or 4 billion and all you got me was the reauthorization of the Clean Air Act—and by the way a very poor reauthorization—I'd fire you. If you look at the money that goes into the environmental movement, including the animal-welfare and animal-protection movement, you are looking at billions of dollars and billions of contributors. And if you look at the actual results—and please, let's not talk about documents. There are goals for 2050, for 2075. Goal-oriented legislation perpetrates a pernicious fraud on the American public, which the Clean Air Act and the Clean Water Act both did. Agenda 21 is a nonsense document, and so are the biodiversity conventions, which basically allow multinational companies to patent genetic resources around the world.

Patrick Michaels: Do you believe that the Clean Air Act of 1990 will have no effect even with the $42 billion annual cost that begins in about 1996?

Andrew Kimbrell: It will have some effect, but it was an extremely inefficient act from the beginning. Goal-oriented legislation is always going to be inefficient. What you need to do is actually say *how* something is to be done, not just *that* it is going to be done.

Patrick Michaels: About this idea that nothing has been done: $600 million a year is what is voluntarily contributed to the sixteen largest environmental organizations. How can this huge lobby be so incompetent?

Andrew Kimbrell: That's a good question. I wish I knew the answer.

Robert Nelson: Charles Rubin used the word *everythingism.* Another word he could use would be *religion,* for in a sense religion is about everything, or about trying to interpret everything. What environmentalism is doing in American life is raising a lot of basically religious questions that have been around for a long time. It represents a kind of revival of interest in certain kinds of religious questions. Why not use the word *religion,* then? My answer would be that environmentalists didn't want to conduct that religious discussion in traditional religious terms. Many of them were not Christian and were uncomfortable with that language and framework. And so they had to create a new vocabulary, the vocabulary of environmentalism. Christians who use these terms should be aware that this vocabulary was specifically designed to avoid having a Christian context.

A strain of environmentalism that is central to a lot of its political activities and explains a lot of its influence in the United States is the part that derives from Calvinism, Puritanism, and American Protestantism in general. It has, in its new secular vocabulary, picked up a number of Protestant themes. For instance, the theme that mankind is the cancer of the earth—it's a very Calvinist kind of way of thinking about the world. Human beings are deeply and innately evil. Also, if you read Calvin you find a lot of language about nature being the messenger of God, nature shining lights that reveal to mankind the presence of God and some of the significance of God. And where has environmentalism succeeded in Europe? Basically in the Protestant countries—Germany, Scandinavia, to some extent in England. There has been much less interest in Italy, Spain, and France. You could develop an argument with respect to environmentalism along the lines of Max Weber's arguments about capitalism.

If when environmentalists march into the halls of Congress and ask to create wilderness areas they are really asking to create a cathedral, a place where they can practice their religion, where does that leave us with respect to separation of church and state?

Ronald Bailey: For a while I was in graduate school at the City University of New York in political science, which was something like what the higher party school in Moscow must have been like. I think I was the only non-socialist to go there in ten years. It was a most interesting time to watch my fellow students and the faculty, because socialism was collapsing, and all of a sudden environmentalism went way up in popularity. All of a sudden new groups were being formed, and they were talking about green socialism. There is among the environmentalists a group of people who are radically alienated from capitalist, industrial society. Once they hoped with Marxism that capitalist society would strangle on its own internal contradictions; now they want it to strangle on its own wastes.

Of course there's a diversity of opinion among environmentalists. There's a diversity of opinion among Marxists. But if you read the major people who are influencing the movement—Gore, Snyder, Hansen—you become very aware of this totalizing vision that Charles Rubin described.

Ron Sider implied something that I found astonishing: that given the choice between increased affluence and the continued existence of spotted owls, he'd choose spotted owls. The fact of the matter is that affluence saves human lives. Wealthier is healthier. Wealthier is less risky, almost without limits. If you think there are some limits, I challenge you to specify what they are. Affluence is a human good almost without limits. I don't mean to be idolatrous. I choose affluence, I like it, it makes my life better, it gives me more choice, it allows me to get off the dairy farm I grew up on and take part in discussions like this one. It's a good thing.

Jo Kwong: I find it hard to sort out the continued resistance to the idea of markets, the view of commodities as very negative things. One of the reasons why I believe in the market so strongly is that it allows for the individual expression of values. If people in a community believe that solar technology is great—it's low tech, it's low capital, it's community based—then, if we have a system of property rights in place, the community can bring in solar technology.

What level of bureaucracy would be required to allocate goods and services if there were no market, no institution where people can say, This is how I value something and I am willing to trade this for that? Of course there are limits to markets. When I say that I'm a diehard market person I usually am asked, Well, what about the markets for body parts or children or animal eyes? Of course we need a framework of cultural values. We need that regardless of what sort of institutional system we adopt.

Stan LeQuire: I appreciated Charles Rubin's point about looking in our own backyard. There is something within the human psyche that causes us to focus on Out There, on rainforests in South America rather than on our own backyard. Rubin comments that a lot of problems "can be addressed by individual efforts or voluntary associations." I'd like some examples of this kind of grassroots activity.

Charles Rubin: People decide that the little stream that runs through their community needs to be cleaned up, so they spend a day pulling out the old tires and other junk in the stream and along its banks. Other people take the next step: they try to work with water authorities to improve the quality of the water. If you're concerned about a particular piece of land, buy it and take care of it. That's the sort of thing that is very appropriate. But the extremes have dominated the debate. *Fifty Things You Can Do to Save the Earth*—why does a book have to have that kind of title? What you do doesn't count if you are not "saving the earth." I don't want people to be dissatisfied after a day's work of cleaning up the stream. I want them to say, Yes, we did a damned good job. Let's keep at it, and let's see what other sorts of things we can do along the same lines.

Andrew Kimbrell: One of the species that I have a great love for is the striped bass. The striped bass was becoming virtually extinct in the Northeast. Finally, several states got together and put in a 36-inch limit on catching. Fishermen joined with environmentalists in a coalition to get this legislation passed. That 36-inch limit was a disaster, of course, for some commercial fisherman, but it did absolutely save a species. We need a mix of private and public efforts, some working within the regulatory system, some working in private. That's a rational and reasonable approach, rather than saying no government or no private sector.

Thomas Derr: I think it is useful to identify trends and hence to talk in general terms about phenomenona that are actually rather disparate. I think it's useful to say that there are anti-human tendencies in the environmental movement, even if they surface only at the extremes. These tendencies arise out of the presuppositions of the movement, and it's important to identify them even if they don't apply directly to everyone who think's he's an environmentalist.

On the local versus the more regional level of attack on the problems: the great principle of subsidiarity is the best thing to apply here. That is, you do something at the lowest level at which it can be done.

That certainly is true of the environment, but there are a lot of things that can't be done at the local level.

Susan Drake: People often tend to think the truth is located between two extremes. I don't find that that is the pursuit of truth. You don't necessarily find the truth between two extremes.

The current environmental movement is dying, if not already dead. The reason why, in my view, is that environmentalists have separated the human from the natural. They haven't been able to create a paradigm that touches the fundamental values of American society. The term *environment* focuses attention solely on the natural world, rather than directing us to care for both the human and the natural creation.

Richard Baer: We have talked a lot about markets vs. government, choice vs. regulation. I think one of the really serious problems we face today is that we have raised a generation of children so self-preoccupied that they are not going to function well as either capitalists or bureaucrats. Adam Smith *does* have his hook on moral theory, he does say that capitalism won't work without people of integrity. Bureaucracies fail simply because people are far more interested in their own prestige and promotions than in doing the work. Wendell Berry asks in *The Unsettling of America:* Why do we think we will have fidelity toward the land if we don't have fidelity in our marriages? Why do we think we can be utterly exploitative in our human relations and then turn around and be environmental saints? Educational theorists talk about liberal "neutrality." We know that education is not ever neutral. There is a tremendous push toward relativism, toward a subjectivism focused on the self. The decision-making units that are used in many classes in the lower grades basically tell the child, in regard to such things as drugs and sex: It's your personal decision. It's not your parents' decision or your church's decision, it's yours. Our educational structures push us toward the lowest common denominator in dealing with values.

How can we have a thick enough moral community to be able to educate our children to develop the character, the commitments, that will go beyond this kind of self-centeredness that is endemic in our schools, our television, and in most of the rest of our culture? I don't think that either markets or bureaucracies are going to work very well if citizens are not able to reclaim the educational structures. Even at the university level, when it comes to traditional Jewish or Christian values, there is massive censorship by omission in almost all of our major universities. We have such thin moral communities in education that it just is not possible to develop the kind of character that makes both bureaucracies and markets work well.

Richard Land: I think there is clearly a sort of secularized perversion of the Protestant impulse that has been seized upon, first of all by utopians of a McGovern type in the 1960s and 1970s, and now by environmentalists. When George McGovern was running for president, he said something like this: "I was so liberated when I realized that I could keep the desire to help people that I got from my Methodist pastor/father and jettison all the religious stuff." That is probably as good a one-sentence definition of McGovern and all those who have been badly influenced by him and the movement he represents as I can articulate. Stephen Carter in his book *The Culture of Disbelief* talks about the trivialization of religious conviction, particularly any kind of traditional religious conviction. The different elites in our culture—and there are lots of elites, some on the left and some on the right—have conspired, both consciously and unconsciously, as Dr. Carter points out in his book, to trivialize religious conviction and to drive it to the margins of our culture. The connection between religious conviction and the ideas that we deal with has been severed. We breathe in the air of this culture, we imbibe through the pores in our skin the idea that there should be no connection between our religious convictions, whatever they are, and our ideas about a whole host of issues.

Civil rights was not an issue of right and left, it was an issue of right and wrong. It was a religious and a moral issue. When we decided that racism was wrong, we made it illegal, at least in our public institutions.

We have to find a way to rejuvenate some sort of common public educational system, because no civilization is ever more than one generation away from barbarism if it fails to pass on its culture to the next generation. What I see happening in this country in too many ways is instead of *e pluribus unum,* "out of many one," Al Gore's mistranslation of it: "out of one many."

Fred Smith: Heterogeneous America early on recognized that in a world where there were extremely strong conflicts and where the religious wars of Europe were a recent part of our heritage, we had best find ways of separating traditional religious values from the political world, of separating church and state. In the environmental field, our mistake has been to massively expand the political role while at the same time weakening the private-sector alternative. Today environmental policy is political policy. The role of the dedicated environmentalist is to lobby Congress for more laws, more power to the bureaucrats. There's more concern in the environmental movement about the Clean Air Act than about clean air, about the Endangered Species Act than about endangered species. How are we going to change that and seek new opportunities?

Let's divide the environmental movement into two parts: the disaffected individuals who see environmentalism as a way of rectifying an inherently unjust society, and those individuals concerned about pollution and biodiversity loss. What strategies could be used to address these concerns privately?

The people who want to save the environment have greatly misunderstood what happened historically in America. American common law's remedies against pollution were sabotaged by the same progressive movement that led to collectivism in other areas. Property rights were ignored when they might block economic progress. We need to revisit those progressive policies and recognize that markets didn't fail, property rights didn't fail, so much as they were sabotaged. This history is relatively unknown. Progressive-era policies also blocked the evolution of institutional arrangements that would have allowed private parties to advance environmental values. We froze one-third of the United States in political ownership. We banned private ownership of wildlife. We advanced the silly concept that trees should have standing, rather than seeking creative alternative ways of ensuring that individuals could act as stewards, standing behind trees, whales, and all the other things we care about. If we revisit those decisions, we might well decide that the private sector has a much richer role to play in protecting environmental resources than we thought.

The private environmental vision is very much like the private schooling vision: not to cripple the political sector but to open up alternatives where other value perspectives can reemerge and allow a richer array of choices. The environment is too important to leave to the bureaucrats.

2

The Climate-Change Debacle: The Perils of Politicizing Science

Patrick J. Michaels

During the past decade much has been said about the "greenhouse effect," whereby a portion of the heat energy radiated from the earth is recycled near the earth's surface; carbon dioxide, methane, water vapor, and other gases in the atmosphere prevent some of this energy from directly passing out to space. The combustion of fossil fuels (petroleum, coal, natural gas) is the primary cause of the increases in these gases. The enhanced greenhouse effect, also known as "global warming," potentially represents the greatest environmental disturbance ever associated with our species.

Concern that climate may be changing and that humans beings are the cause is not new. Thomas Jefferson hypothesized that the deforestation of the Mid-Atlantic region resulted in changed wind patterns as far west as the Blue Ridge Mountains. (He was wrong.) A hundred years later, the British physicist John Tyndall performed pioneering laboratory experiments on the absorption of infrared energy by certain constituents of the atmosphere, including carbon dioxide and water vapor. In 1896, the Swedish chemist Svante Arrhenius generalized Tyndall's findings to the globe and concluded that if the atmospheric

---

Patrick J. Michaels is associate professor of environmental sciences at the University of Virginia. He is also the Virginia state climatologist.

carbon dioxide were to double, the mean temperature of the planet would rise some five degrees Celsius.

Half a century later, the invention of the digital computer allowed Arrhenius's findings to be generalized to specific regions and seasons. The result was "General Circulation Models" (GCMs), which can simulate the atmosphere disturbed by an enhanced greenhouse effect. For estimating future climatic change, these simulations form the only quantitative scientific formulation of sufficient resolution that does not rely upon past temperature records or geological results of limited accuracy. They are the basis for the United Nations Framework Convention on Climate Change, the "Rio Treaty," described below. The GCMs, and the rather dire pictures they paint, are the most important component of the call for action on global warming.

Rarely acknowledged in any debate are several important points concerning the substantial limitations and unreliability of the simulations. This omission probably occurs, not out of an attempt to mislead the public, but because many in the environmental community lack the training required to appreciate some important subtleties.

The primitive mid-1980s versions of these models were the ones most featured in congressional hearings about global warming that began around 1985. These models predicted, on the average, that the mean surface temperature of the earth will warm up 4.2°C (7.6°F) if the concentration of atmospheric carbon dioxide is doubled. In the high latitudes of the Northern Hemisphere, the projected winter changes average around 8°C (14.4°F), and in some areas are nearly 20°C (36°F). The most recent generation of these models predicts a somewhat reduced average warming of 3.4° C (6.1°F) for a doubling of CO_2.

The Fudge Factors

In 1994 three MIT scientists investigated what *Science* magazine now refers to as the "fudge factors" in these climate models. Left to their own devices and working solely with known scientific principles, the models simulate a climate that simply does not exist. To correct for this, modelers introduced artificial changes in the amount of warming radiation moving poleward. Removing the "fudge factor" after getting the "right" answer then resulted in unreliable forecasts of the future (which should come as no surprise).

Consider one of the most advanced American GCMs, the coupled atmosphere-ocean model published in the August 1991 *Journal of Climate.*[1] In order to achieve a realistic nineteenth-century climate, this GCM assumes that the energy coming from the sun is some 20 watts per square meter less than it really is. Normally, around half of the sun's radiation actually goes to warm the atmosphere as it passes through, so the effect of unrealistically decreasing the sun's output by 20 watts actually translates to about 10 watts per square meter at the surface of the planet. But enhancing the greenhouse effect by doubling the carbon dioxide in the atmosphere is equivalent to increasing radiation at the earth's surface by about 4.0 watts per square meter. Consequently, the "adjustment" factor used to get the right temperature before an increase in CO_2 is factored in is in fact over twice as large as the change expected to be caused by a change in CO_2!

Thus we cannot simulate the current climate from known scientific principles. Therefore the question "how much do we expect the climate to change?" becomes impossible to answer with confidence. In recognition of this problem, a facile switch was made in all GCMs that few people outside the climate-modeling community are aware of: model output is presented, not as the expected change from, say, the current climate, or even the global climate around 1900, but as the difference between two model runs, one using "$1 \times CO_2$" and the other using "$2 \times CO_2$." The "forecast" is actually one model, complete with the systematic errors described above (and many more), subtracted from an equally flawed "background" model.

Imagine that today's weather forecast for the Corn Belt was, say, ten degrees too hot, but that the forecaster knew it and arbitrarily subtracted away the error. This is what occurs in climate models. In the weather-forecast situation, all subsequent computer products that were made public, ranging from the probability of severe thunderstorms to the agricultural forecast for crop spraying, would appear reasonable; yet would they be driven by a model that was producing known and large errors of agricultural consequence. Knowing that an error of this magnitude was lurking in the weather forecast, would society make expensive plans as a result?

Similar and unfortunately very real problems (unlike the fabricated one in our weather-forecasting example) are present in the GCMs, and, on the basis of these faulty models, we have signed a treaty that has the potential to force the most dramatic managing of the American economy in the nation's history.

It is not surprising that the amount of global warming predicted by the average of current GCMs—3.4°C for a doubling of CO_2—is in the range of Arrhenius's original calculation. But he also calculated that the temperature rise at the point half-way to a doubling of pre-industrial CO_2, which is where we stand today, would be 3.0°C. Even scientists who are not fluent with the temperature history of the planet know that it has not warmed nearly this amount since the enhancement began.

Examining the Assertions

A forecast is nothing but a scientific hypothesis, and hypotheses stand or fall on objective fact rather than on other computer simulations. Let us look at the assertions that accompany the GCM forecasts:

1. The history of climatic warming should be consonant with the enhancement of the greenhouse effect.
2. Water warms more slowly than land. Therefore the Southern Hemisphere, which is mostly water at its surface, should warm much more slowly than the Northern Hemisphere, which contains almost all of the planetary landmass.
3. Warming should be greatest in the high latitudes of both hemispheres.

The combination of several greenhouse-enhancing gases (carbon dioxide, methane, chlorofluorocarbons, nitrous oxide, in descending order) has raised the CO_2 level in the atmosphere from the natural 270 parts per million to approximately 410 (expressed as CO_2 equivalents to allow for the different characteristics of the various greenhouse gases). Almost half of this increase has been since World War II.

Approximately 13 per cent of the current "warming potential" arises from chlorofluorocarbons (CFCs). These compounds, once used widely as aerosol propellants and refrigerants, are being phased out of production in accordance with the Montreal Protocol on substances that deplete stratospheric ozone. They are very effective greenhouse gases; had they been left unchecked, their increase would have made them responsible for 20 per cent of the warming potential by the middle of the next century. Although the elimination of CFCs clearly will reduce the rise in the greenhouse effect, the United Nations does not take account of this in its reckoning.

Projections vs. Observations

The surface-temperature histories for the Southern and Northern Hemispheres published by the U.S. Department of Energy support a rise of 0.45°C plus or minus .10° in the last 100 years, on a global scale.[2] But the mid-1980s GCM projections produce an expected warming—given the observed trace-gas change—of around 2.0°C.

In addition, the "water" (Southern) hemisphere should warm up more slowly. While most of its measuring stations are on land, the fact that so much of the hemisphere is water means there is more oceanic influence on the record there than occurs in the Northern Hemisphere. However, the Southern Hemisphere shows the *greater* "greenhouse-like" effect.

Trend analysis of the global surface-temperature records demonstrates, in a statistical sense, that much of the observed warming was realized prior to 1945.[3] In 1945 the concentration of greenhouse gases was approximately 310ppm, compared to today's 410; only a quarter of the enhancement of the greenhouse gases (from the natural 270ppm) that we observe today had occurred. This means, then, that there has been relatively little additional warming during the period in which three-quarters of the greenhouse-effect change has taken place.

Even the United Nations concurs. In the famous 1990 report of the Intergovernmental Panel on Climate Change, page 246 makes it quite apparent that during the last fifty years the global temperature has *never* been on the warming track projected by the mid-1980s GCMs.[4] The report states that if the rise in twentieth-century temperatures were caused only by changing the greenhouse effect, then the net rise for doubled CO_2 would be only 1.3°C.

Furthermore, it is not known how much of the warming measured in surface-based records is attributable to the "urban warming effect," a common problem that results because cities tend to grow around weather-observing stations. Satellite data, which began in 1979, show no statistically significant warming of either hemisphere between 1979 and 1995, though the ground-based records for the same period in the Southern Hemisphere do show some warming. Figures 1 and 2 show these hemispheric satellite records, with the warming predicted by GCMs superimposed.

Figure 1

NORTHERN HEMISPHERE, 1979-1994:
Observed Temperatures (Satellite) and GCM Predicted Temperatures

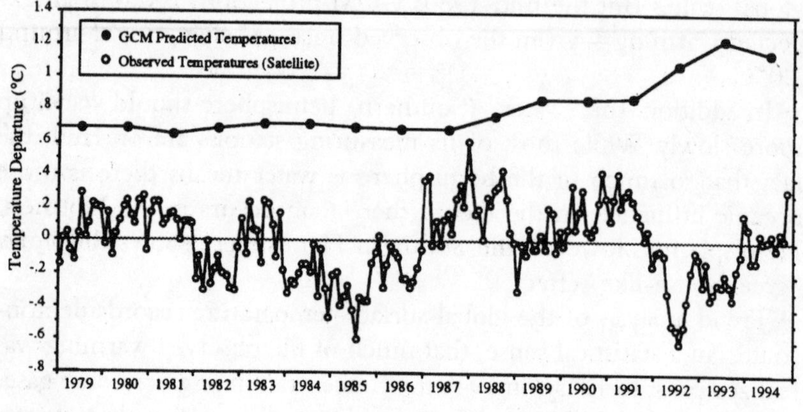

Figure 2

SOUTHERN HEMISPHERE, 1979-1994:
Observed Temperatures (Satellite) and GCM Predicted Temperatures

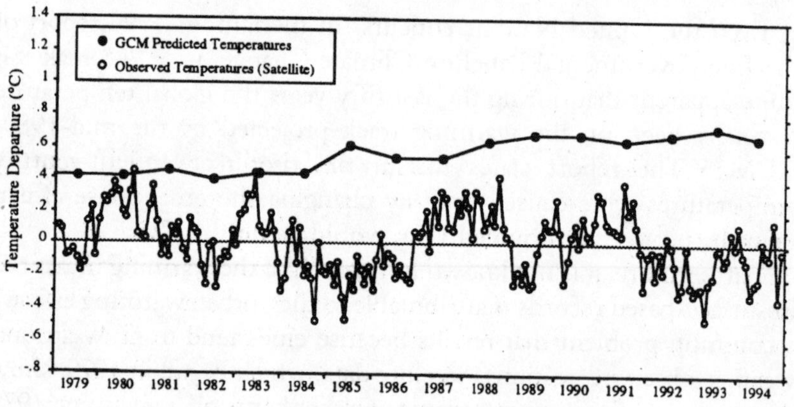

Source: The predicted temperatures in Figures 1 and 2 are from the GCM of S. Manabe et al., *Journal of Climate* 4 (1991): 785-818.

The surface-based records also show very little difference in the overall ground-based temperature changes in the two hemispheres, even though the predominance of land in the Northern Hemisphere should result in a more rapid warming.

Polar temperature histories are also inconsistent with the prime assertions about climatic change. In the coupled ocean-atmosphere GCM of Manabe et al. in which the greenhouse effect changes more realistically than in previous models, the high latitudes of the Northern Hemisphere are predicted to have warmed by 2.0°C since 1950.[5] But the Department of Energy compendium of temperature records indicates a rapid rise in Arctic temperatures *prior* to most of the greenhouse-gas emissions. In most polar records, the rise in temperature is followed by a decline, from the 1940s to the mid-70s, similar in proportion to the rise.

All GCMs suggest that the polar warming will be magnified in winter. Nonetheless, there has been a substantial decline in winter temperatures over the Atlantic Arctic since 1920,[6] and there has been no change in polar night temperatures averaged over Antarctica.[7] Kahl et al. found no net warming of the Arctic, and there was even some evidence for a cooling of winter temperatures.[8] Conversely, Kalkstein et al. have documented that, while there has been no net warming of the North American Arctic, the coldest air masses, whose mean surface temperatures are approximately -40°, have warmed some two degrees.[9]

Is the Warming "Hidden"?

Most scientists who are conversant with both the GCMs and the temperature histories now acknowledge the discrepancies between greenhouse assertions about climatic warming and the observed temperatures. As a result, some have argued that the predicted effect has been obscured by the "anti-greenhouse" products of combustion, such as sulfate aerosol.[10] If this is true, then the GCMs should perform significantly better in sulfate-free environments, such as the Southern Hemisphere or both polar regions, and poorer in the sulfate regions of eastern North America, Europe, and East Asia.

Sulfate aerosols hypothetically counter greenhouse warming by increasing the reflectivity of the lower atmosphere (via direct aerosol backscattering) so that more heat is radiated away from the earth's surface, or by serving as condensation nuclei that increase the amount of low-level (stratiform) clouds. In either case the prime effect is reflective, so the sulfate effect should be most pronounced in the summer, when the clouds have the longest length of day to reflect radiation.

In a recent paper, we examined the detailed behavior of the *Journal of Climate* GCM cited earlier. We divided our study into the polar regions, the earth's hemispheres, and the sulfate region of the Northern Hemisphere.[11] Studies were separated into winter and summer. If sulfates were mitigating the warming predicted by the model, the following should be observed:

1. The model should perform worst where sulfates are highly concentrated.
2. The model should perform better in the Southern Hemisphere, as almost all sulfate emissions are in the Northern Hemisphere.
3. The model should perform best in the polar regions, which are virtually sulfate-free.

In general, we found that we could no longer entertain the primary hypothesis that underlies policy proposals on global warming: that the *observed* patterns of climatic change resemble those that were *predicted*.

Further, we found no support for the hypothesis that the countereffect of sulfate aerosol is a sufficient cause of this failure. None of the three hypotheses concerning GCM behavior difference over the sulfate region, between hemispheres, and between the poles and the hemispheres is supported by the data. In fact, in the sulfate region the only patterns in which what was forecast resembled what was observed occurred in the summer—when the model should be most compromised by sulfates. In this case, the model correctly captures the statistically most important pattern of observed climatic change, thus *countering* the sulfate hypothesis.

The addition to a GCM of any type of parameter that reduces the predicted warming, particularly in the mid-latitudes of the Northern Hemisphere (where the sulfate density is greatest), will increase the correspondence between the model and reality. Thus we can expect a number of simulations to appear in which reflectivity or low cloud cover is increased in these regions, and consequent reduced warming will be initially forecast, followed by a more rapid warming as the compensating parameter is removed. But our results suggest that calculating this compensation in a sulfate-region GCM, as was done by Hansen et al.,[12] will make the GCM "right" for the wrong reason, for its failure was in fact greater in the sulfate-free polar region. This alteration of GCMs will make them even more unreliable as estimators of future climate than they had been in their more pristine state.

The Rio Treaty

Most nations in the world have ratified the 1992 United Nations Framework Convention on Climate Change, first signed in Rio de Janeiro at the Earth Summit. The stated purpose of the treaty is to "achieve . . . stabilization of greenhouse gas concentrations in the atmosphere at a level that would prevent dangerous anthropogenic interference with the climate system."

So we have agreed to stabilize greenhouse gases at a level that would prevent man's "dangerous interference" with the climate. But GCMs indicate that we have already interfered with the climate in a "dangerous" fashion, while the observed data are in large part counter to GCM forecasts. If we are at the "danger" level, the required reduction in greenhouse-gas emissions from today's level would be 60 to 80 per cent. In the United States, for example, this would require emission rates somewhere around the 1930 level. In developing nations, there would be virtually no fossil-fuel combustion.

No one knows how to do this. In October 1993, President Clinton announced a "voluntary" program, known as the "Climate Change Action Plan," to meet one goal of the Rio Treaty: the reduction of emissions to 1990 levels by the year 2000. Even if successful, this plan will not advance the overall treaty objective, because it will not contribute to "stabilization of greenhouse gas concentrations." All it says is that we will reduce our emissions to 1990 levels. In 1990, greenhouse-gas concentrations were increasing by approximately 25 parts per million in equivalent CO_2 every ten years; reducing emissions to that level merely maintains that level of increase, rather than "stabilizing" the concentrations.

Even though the GCM forecasts appear to have overestimated warming, we can use them to estimate how much warming this policy will prevent. If their forecasts are assumed to be correct it is a very small amount: if all the nations succeeded in implementing Clinton's program, the amount of warming that would be prevented through the year 2025 would be approximately 0.2°C.

The "voluntary" program, not surprisingly, is failing. Writing in Spring 1994 in the newsletter *Energy, Economics and Climate Change*, analyst Nick Sundt calculated that, by the end of 1993, U.S. emissions had reached levels that would have occurred in 1996 without any attempt to limit them. According to Howard Geller of the American Council for an Energy Efficient Economy, this resulted because of "rapid economic growth, low energy prices, and unfavorable weather" (meaning the cold winter of 1993-94, not global warming).

The objective of the Rio Treaty, as stated above, is to stabilize greenhouse-gas concentrations in the atmosphere "at a level that would prevent dangerous anthropogenic interference with the climate system." More important are some provisions in its various articles. A number of these are quoted and (in most cases) commented on below.

From Article 3: Principles

ARTICLE 3.1 and ARTICLE 3.2: "The Parties should protect the climate system . . . on the basis of equity. . . . Accordingly, the developed country Parties should take the lead in combating climate change and the adverse effects thereof" (3.1). "The specific needs and special circumstances of developing country Parties . . . should be given full consideration" (3.2).

Comment: Twenty-five nations with a high Gross Domestic Product (Russia and the other former Soviet states are notably excepted) will have the goal of reducing emissions to 1990 levels by the year 2000. (This will hereafter be referred to as the 1990/2000 goal.) All others, whose emissions are growing at a much faster rate than those of the high-GDP states, are not constrained by any goal, even though their emissions will be the largest of any group of nations by early in the twenty-first century.

ARTICLE 3.3: "Where there are threats of serious or irreversible damage, lack of full scientific certainty should not be used as a reason for postponing . . . measures [to anticipate, prevent, or minimize the causes of climate change and mitigate its adverse effects]."

Comment: As long as an argument can be made that there is some "threat" of serious damage, action may not be postponed despite the existence of scientific data that may not be consistent with that threat. Signatories can therefore be forced to reduce emissions in spite of any evidence that it might not be necessary.

ARTICLE 3.4: "Policies and measures to protect the climate system . . . should be integrated with national development programmes."

Comment: The U.N. assumes that all nations centrally plan their development.

From Article 4: Commitments

ARTICLE 4.1a: "[The signatories will] develop . . . national inventories of anthropogenic emissions by sources and removals by sinks of all greenhouse gases not controlled by the Montreal Protocol."

Comment: This important clause was designed to keep the nations (notably the United States) that have produced considerable amounts of chlorofluorocarbons (CFCs), which are being eliminated by the Montreal Protocol for stratospheric ozone protection, from counting those eliminations as reductions in global-warming potential. Yet they *are* reductions in warming potential, and the United States could easily meet the 1990/2000 goal with the phase-out of CFCs that has already been mandated by Congress.

ARTICLE 4.1c: "Promote and cooperate in the development, application and diffusion, *including transfer,* of technologies . . . that . . . reduce or prevent anthropogenic emissions of greenhouse gases [emphasis added]."

Comment: This treaty can mandate the *transfer* (which does not mean the sale) of energy technologies to nations that are relatively inefficient. The result of this clause has been to enlist the support of many lobbying organizations associated with energy technology, because, if the technology is "transferred" without cost to a foreign country, it will still have to be purchased here—by taxpayer dollars—before it is transferred.

ARTICLE 4.1i: "Promote and cooperate in education . . . and . . . awareness related to climate change and encourage the widest participation in this process, including that of non-governmental organizations."

Comment: Virtually all the "non-governmental organizations" represented at the Rio Earth Summit (where the treaty was signed) were either environmental groups, such as Greenpeace, or group-rights advocates. The signatories are therefore bound to "encourage . . . participation" in the environmental educational process by these groups.

ARTICLE 4.2a: "[Each of the signatory developed countries shall] adopt national policies and take corresponding measures on the mitigation of climate change, by limiting its anthropogenic emissions of greenhouse gases and protecting and enhancing its greenhouse sinks and reservoirs."

Comment: Here the signatories commit themselves to reducing greenhouse-gas emissions and "protecting and enhancing" sinks, which by and large means forested land. In other words, the developed nations may violate this treaty if they do not limit emissions or if they do not increase their forested land. This article is an open invitation for environmental organizations to bring suit against the signatories, as has already occurred in Australia.

ARTICLE 4.2b: "[Each of the signatory developed countries] in order to promote progress towards this end [Article 4.2a] shall communicate, within six months of the entry into force of the convention . . . detailed information on its policies on greenhouse gases not controlled by the Montreal Protocol [see 4.1a, above] . . . with the aim of returning to [the 1990/2000 goal]."

Comment: This meeting took place in Berlin in March 1995. Signatories agreed to set specific emission reductions (beyond the 1990/2000 goal) at Tokyo in 1997. This commits the United States to some type of increased reduction, but specific targets and scheduling were not announced.

ARTICLE 4.3: "The developed country Parties . . . shall provide *new and additional* financial resources to meet the agreed full costs incurred by the developing countries under Article 12, Paragraph 1 [emphasis added]. They shall also provide such financial resources, including for the transfer of technology, needed by the developing country parties to meet the agreed full incremental costs of implementing measures that are covered by Paragraph 1 of this article. The implementation of these commitments shall take into account the need for adequacy . . . in the flow of funds and the importance of appropriate burden sharing among the developed country parties."

Comment: Article 12, Paragraph 1, states, among other things, that each signatory will communicate a description of steps taken to implement the convention. Article 4.3 can therefore be used to compel the developed nations to pay for whatever the developing nations say they must do to comply with the convention.

ARTICLE 4.4: "The developed country Parties . . . shall *also* assist the developing country Parties that are particularly vulnerable to the adverse effects of climate change in meeting costs of adaptation to those adverse effects [emphasis added]."

Comment: Because no climate model can confirm or deny that a particular phenomenon—say, increased drought frequency in Sahelian Africa—is related to greenhouse emissions, developed nations may simply assert such a claim and demand compensation based on this treaty.

ARTICLE 4.5: "The developed country Parties . . . shall take all practicable steps to promote, facilitate and *finance* . . . the transfer of, or access to, environmentally sound technologies and know-how to other Parties, particularly developing country Parties . . . [emphasis added]."

Comment: This important clause states that the developed nations will subsidize the purchase of technologies and "know-how" (which may mean patented processes) to other nations. This means, in the United States, that companies that produce more efficient energy technology will have that technology exported at taxpayer expense. It is therefore not surprising that an industrial consortium has arisen that strongly supports the treaty, despite its ultimate goal. This clause can require that public monies be used to purchase privately held technology that is ultimately given or lent to Third World nations.

ARTICLE 4.6: "In the implementation of their commitments . . . , a certain degree of flexibility shall be allowed by the Conference of the Parties to the Parties included in Annex I undergoing the transition to a market economy. . . ."

Comment: The parties listed in Annex I, those to be allowed "flexibility," are Belarus, Bulgaria, Czechoslovakia, Estonia, Hungary, Latvia, Lithuania, Poland, Romania, Russia, and Ukraine. And so these articles really apply only to the industrialized democracies; the formerly Communist countries are relieved of their responsibilities.

ARTICLE 6(a)(i): "The parties shall promote . . . the development and implementation of educational and public awareness programmes on climate change and its effects and (iii) public participation in addressing climate change and its effects and developing adequate responses."

From Article 21: Interim Arrangements

ARTICLE 21.2: "The head of the interim secretariat . . . will cooperate closely with the Intergovernmental Panel on Climate Change (IPCC) to ensure that the Panel can respond to the need for objective scientific and technical advice. Other relevant scientific bodies could also be consulted."

Comment: The IPCC, a United Nations entity that is used to define scientific "consensus," can serve as the sole scientific advisory panel for this treaty.

From Article 25: Withdrawal

ARTICLE 25.1: "At any time after three years from the date on which the Convention has entered into force . . . a . . . party may withdraw . . . by giving written notification. . . ."

Comment: Any of the signatories, including the United States, can legally withdraw from the Framework Convention on Climate Change by sending a letter after March 21, 1997.

Future Policy

The Clinton administration has stated that the commitments made in the Rio Treaty are not adequate because they do not address what will happen beyond the year 2000. Indeed, as noted above, if the "danger" argument is cited, the commitments are clearly insufficient and will have little effect on the predicted global warming. In early 1995 Germany proposed a 20 per cent reduction in emissions (from 1990 levels) by the year 2005 as the new goal for the treaty. The DRI —McGraw Hill econometric firm has estimated that by the year 2020 this would cost $2,500 per capita per year (in 1989 dollars) in the United States. Ironically, this reduction in emissions would have only a modest effect on global warming.

We have entered into a treaty designed to prevent a "dangerous" climate change that is predicted by models that aren't working, and we have produced a policy that cannot succeed. How did this happen?

It seems obvious that there is a considerable disconnection between early forecasts and recent observations of climate change. Yet GCM forecasts were at the core of the 1990 "Report of the Intergovernmental Panel on Climate Change" of the United Nations Environment Programme, which served as the scientific basis for the Rio Treaty.

As we saw in looking at Article 3.3, "where there are threats of serious or irreversible damage," the signatories may not postpone action on the basis of a "lack of full scientific certainty." Many have taken this to mean that the normal process of verification of hypotheses (that is, of forecasts) by observation is not required before the nations of the world undertake expensive steps to reduce greenhouse emissions.

Why didn't scientists object to this clear perversion of their professional ethic? In my opinion, the answer lies in the nature of science funding. Virtually every active academic researcher in the environmental sciences is supported by the federal government. Large amounts of research support have been directed towards the issue of global climate change. Since this support would stop if the research community were to say that much of the concern about this issue was misplaced, the policy community received little if any signal indicating that the models were not being verified by observed data.

Diversification: A Solution?

The current situation resulted in large part because scientists are forced to work in a "single provider" research funding system. All of the imbalances that attend a monopoly can be expected to occur: politicization, disequilibrium between true and perceived need, and disproportionate funding of those who express agreement with the monopoly's goals. Because this monopoly is publicly funded and is administered by agencies that require congressional oversight, there is certain to be some political bias with respect to the programs that receive the most funding.

Particularly with applied research, it was not always the case that funding came from a single provider, the federal government. In fact, the federalization of science was relatively inconsequential until the advent of the Manhattan Project, which built the atomic bomb during World War II. Before that, most science was funded by industry, either in-house or at universities. The change from private to public funding was seen by many as a good thing because it gave scientists some freedom from the presumed biases of industry. As long as there was a reasonable mix of the two sources, some type of competition between biases—industry and federal—could create a fertile mix for scientific progress.

That mix, or dynamic equilibrium, does not exist today in the environmental sciences, particularly with respect to climate change. There is virtually no private funding, and the federal biases are obvious. While serving in the Senate, for example, Albert Gore was chairman of the Subcommittee on Science, Space and Technology, which oversees the budgets of both the National Science Foundation and NASA. It is difficult to envision these agency heads testifying at budget hearings in front of the senator-environmentalist that global climate change is not so important an issue that it merits a substantial increase in their budgets!

The States' Interests

The policies that result from this type of bias are often at odds with the interests of certain states. One would be hard put to imagine, for example, that Virginia, West Virginia, Pennsylvania, and Wyoming—major coal-producing states—would enthusiastically support some type of tax on the carbon content of fuels, which is what *must* ultimately be mandated to reduce emissions enough to stabilize CO_2 concentration at or slightly above the current level.

One solution to the problem of federal-monopoly bias is to encourage the reappearance of the competing-industry bias. However, it would seem inappropriate to foster such an effort at the federal level, because the federal bias would ultimately reappear. Rather, states should undertake such a program.

The 1994 session of the Pennsylvania State Legislature saw the passage of a bill designed to create a bias that would compete with the federal bias on funding for climate research. The Bill, called the "Interstate Climate Change Research Act," was passed by the legislature but vetoed by the governor, who said he was committed to funding no new programs during that legislative cycle. (A similar bill was introduced in the 1995 Illinois legislature.)

The Pennsylvania bill had some interesting provisions. It pointed out that climate change could be either deleterious or beneficial, that a great deal of uncertainty surrounds the issue, that the cost of regulation to inhibit prospective changes may be severe, that the impact of regulation would fall disproportionately, and that "certain states may have a differential interest in this issue between them and the federal government." The proposed research would address both negative and positive aspects of climate change in an evenhanded fashion. Funding would originate from for-profit corporations that could reduce their state tax burden by an equivalent amount.

The intent of the Pennsylvania bill was clearly to encourage private industry to fund a basic research pool on climate change. If industry perceived that its contributions were not being well spent (i.e., were not funding research that was appropriate for their bias), then it is likely that their financial support would cease.

It will be interesting to see whether analogous legislation will be submitted in other states that are particularly affected by climate-change regulation.

A Modest Proposal

We have sown the wind—making politics the prime determinant of scientific research targets, using planned science as a vehicle for national planning—and we are now reaping the whirlwind. The political recognition has begun that perhaps federal management is not the only solution to our scientific problems—that, in fact, a single-provider federal science system necessarily produces skewed results and consequent bad policy.

The climate-change debacle—where politicized science created impossible policy—should serve as a model of what is wrong with government monopolies in the information business. Besides leading the United States to sign a treaty it cannot uphold without disrupting its own energy economy, it is also likely to result in a great deal of public distrust of science in general.

A modest proposal: As a public signal that this will no longer be tolerated, perhaps we should legally withdraw from the Rio Treaty, then disburse treaty costs to the states for enhanced research, and start over with a more diverse science base. That might be one benefit that accrues from the great climate-change debacle.

A Response

Christopher Flavin

One of the things I wonder about when listening to Pat Michaels and his "conservative" supporters is why it is considered conservative to view with complacency the idea of profoundly disrupting the world's atmosphere, while assuming (or hoping) that the consequences will be benign. Most conservatives are risk averse and want to protect what we have. Why then would a conservative go out of his way to dismiss all the scientific evidence pointing to climate change, and search obsessively for bits of data that indicate even the slimmest chance that humanity might survive the unprecedented experiment we are conducting with the earth's atmosphere? Conservatives also consider themselves the custodians of values and ethics. But is it ethical to disrupt the natural world without regard to the impact on our descendants or on Creation itself?

Michaels's debating style is to pick a few holes in the vast body of scientific evidence on climate change and assume that listeners will not notice that most of the evidence remains unchallenged. The enormous complexity and inevitable uncertainty entailed in atmospheric science make this approach an easy one to pursue, but it results in a profoundly incomplete and dangerous view of the climate issue.

Michaels's presentation relies heavily on his opinion that the Global Circulation Models used by scientific teams to understand climate change are inconsistent with the record of actual temperature changes

---

Christopher Flavin is vice-president of the Worldwatch Institute, Washington, D.C. He is co-author, with Nicholas Lenssen, of *Power Surge: A Guide to the Coming Energy Revolution* (Norton, 1994).

in the last century or so. Indeed, all scientists agree that the climate models in use today are imperfect. They do not fully represent the earth's extraordinarily complex atmospheric system, and are not capable of predicting exactly what the climate will be in Washington, D.C., a hundred years from now.

Yet to ignore the climate models because they are not perfect is akin to refusing to have a medical checkup because you can't be sure the doctor will predict precisely what your health will be in the future. Imperfect though they are, the climate models provide invaluable insights into the fundamentals of climate change. It is also notable that there have been substantial improvements in climate modeling in the past few years, so that the latest models are able to emulate the historic climate record much more closely than ever before. These models were also vindicated when the cooling effect of the Mount Pinatubo eruption in the early 1990s closely paralleled the magnitude predicted by climate modelers shortly after the eruption. In 1994, the IPCC released a draft of its second major climate-change assessment, confirming the likelihood of a rapid warming in the coming decade.[1]

Scientists have recently managed to integrate oceanic and atmospheric models, and are now able to incorporate the cooling effect of sulfate aerosols. The model developed by the Hadley Center for Climate Prediction and Research at the Meteorological Office in Bracknell, England, which includes the effects of sulfates, shows that the historic temperature record over the past century correlates very closely with their model's predictions, demonstrating a 0.6° C rise in global temperatures since the onset of the Industrial Revolution.[2] The Max Planck Institute in Germany has used similar data to conclude that there is now a 95 per cent probability that the rise in temperature over the past century is caused by rising concentrations of greenhouse gases.[3] Indeed, even the layman has a hard time accepting the notion that it is a mere coincidence that the ten warmest years in the past century have all occurred since 1980.

Signs of Climate Change

Regional climate changes that have been detected recently are also consistent with the projections of Global Circulation Models. For example, the rapid warming of Antarctica projected by many models has been clearly detected in recent years and is causing deglaciation in some areas. North America, on the other hand, should not be experiencing much warming at this point—as a result of heavy sulfur emissions—which is in fact the case. The rapid warming of Europe in recent decades is also consistent with the climate models.

Other evidence also indicates change. Pine trees in northern Finland have begun a dramatic advance north into tundra areas in apparent response to warmer temperatures—at a rate of about forty meters per year, according to a scientist at the University of Helsinki. In Switzerland and Austria, researchers have documented a rapid retreat of many glaciers, uncovering areas that have been under deep ice for thousands of years. Oceanographers at the Hopkins Institute in Monterey, California, which has been tracking undersea life for sixty years, say that marine snails and other mollusks normally found in warm waters are now expanding their ranges north along the Pacific Coast, while cold-water species retreat.

Climate change is also indicated by a new space-based measuring device—an orbiting radar gun—that during the past three years has been able to detect a small but significant rate of increase in sea level, a trend that is consistent with the thermal expansion that occurs as a result of warming. Scientists have detected other "fingerprints" of climate change that suggest that greenhouse warming is under way. For example, in many parts of the world, tropical corals, which are highly sensitive to water temperature, are dying. Large-scale die-offs of oceanic plankton have also been detected. Health impacts are also being observed, according to some scientists. Researchers at Harvard University believe that recent outbreaks of cholera in South America, Hanta virus in the U.S. Southwest, and pneumonic plague in India may all be connected to rising temperatures.

The timing of the earth's seasons, which is crucial to agriculture, may also be affected. A recent study by David J. Thomson, a scientist at AT&T's Bell Labs, demonstrates a profound shift in the timing of seasons that began in 1940, reversing a pattern of relative stability that had lasted for three hundred years.[4] Dr. Thomson believes there is an extremely high probability that this shift is related to the rapid rise in greenhouse-gas concentrations in recent decades. Another recent study demonstrates that since 1980, the climate of the United States has become substantially more extreme.[5]

Such evidence has convinced Thomas Karl, senior scientist at the National Oceanic and Atmospheric Administration, who was once the darling of Patrick Michaels and other skeptics, that "the data are consistent with the general trends expected from a greenhouse-enhanced atmosphere."[6] He puts the odds that the observed changes are merely a statistical blip at less than 10 per cent. Benjamin Santer, an atmospheric physicist at the Lawrence Berkeley National Laboratory, says, "The circumstantial evidence is getting stronger that the global warming signal is here."[7]

The Danger in Uncertainty

Of course, even as the scientific evidence has strengthened, many aspects of future climate change remain uncertain. But anyone who has studied the way complex science develops—and this is one of the *most* complex fields today—knows that this situation is quite routine. Such complexity almost always entails large degrees of uncertainty. Michaels argues that this uncertainty should make us complacent. According to his theorem, whenever we face a potentially disastrous but uncertain outcome, we should assume the best. "Don't worry, be happy," he tells us.

What the contrarians fail to acknowledge is that the very uncertainty associated with climate change is the biggest danger we face. If we knew for sure whether we will face a 2° or 6° change in global average temperature in the next century, and knew exactly what the effects of that change would be, then we would have a challenging but manageable problem. We could invest in dikes, build new water systems, and perhaps even develop new agricultural technologies.

It is, of course, possible, even likely, that the mean rate of climate change projected by the Intergovernmental Panel on Climate Change (IPCC), the official body of scientists that assesses these issues for the United Nations, will not be realized. Michaels argues that there may be a negative feedback effect, whether it be increased cloud cover or a carbon "sink" that might develop. This cannot be ruled out, but there is also a strong possibility that the rate of climate change and the degree of disruption to human societies might be greater than what the IPCC projects. For example, many scientists are concerned that warming could cause an extensive loss of northern boreal forests, releasing large additional quantities of carbon dioxide.[8] Moreover, warming of the tundra could release large quantities of methane. Either effect could accelerate the rate of climate change beyond what the IPCC is projecting. It is also possible that unanticipated, severe regional effects may occur if, for instance, a major oceanic current were to shift as a result of climate change. Some scientists, for example, hypothesize that a rapid temperature rise could melt both the west and east ice sheets of Antarctica, raising sea levels by up to 150 feet and submerging all the world's coastal cities.[9] In other words, there is a real chance that climate change will be more severe than most scientists currently predict.

We have seen this happen before. In the early 1970s, when the issue of depletion of the ozone layer first emerged as a scientific concern, scientists developed models to anticipate what might happen to the ozone layer as a result of chlorofluorocarbon emissions. Looking back, those models seem incredibly primitive—and ended up being dead wrong. The ozone-depletion problem turned out to be far *more* severe than had been projected. The biggest scientific surprise was the emergence of the "hole" in the ozone layer over Antarctica. This hole was so far from anything scientists had contemplated that when the first satellite observations began to come in showing a severe depletion of the Antarctic ozone layer, scientists assumed it was an artifact of damaged instruments. Only later did they learn that they had discovered a serious new threat.

One of the questions we now face is whether global warming will result in climatic changes that are as dramatic and unwelcome as the hole in the ozone layer. Growing evidence suggests that in the real world, climate change is likely to be spasmodic, unexpected, and so complex that you really have to get into the fields of chaos and complexity theory to begin to understand it. That is, environmental systems can cross thresholds in which a set of gradual trends may be completely disrupted and move in unexpected directions. Extreme climatic events might become more common in a substantially warmer world. These include catastrophic storms of various kinds, particularly those that are fed by warm tropical waters. Droughts could become more severe and last for many years, disrupting agriculture. Heat waves could also kill off crops and forests. The catastrophic wildfires seen in many parts of the world in recent years could also become routine.

As a result of such climatic changes, the coastal development that has expanded so dramatically over the past few decades might suddenly become more vulnerable than before, a problem that is exacerbated by the unprecedented concentrations of human populations in many parts of the world today. Low-lying areas that are dangerous to inhabitants even at current sea levels might become substantially more so with sea levels already rising by 0.3 cm per year. At a time when global food supplies are likely to be relatively tight over the next few decades, climate change could further reduce food security—damaging fisheries as well as crops. And as mentioned earlier, climate change could encourage the spread of deadly infectious diseases.

The Precautionary Principle

Given that even Patrick Michaels cannot deny the possibility of such events, it seems to me that we should invoke what is called "the precautionary principle." That is, we should take prudent steps to ensure that we minimize what could be substantial risks. It is interesting to ask how many of us in our personal or business dealings insist on the kind of certainty Michaels does when considering disastrous outcomes. For example, does a country go to war with absolute certainty of the outcome? Did Bill Gates decide to go into the software business because he knew for sure that he would be more successful than his competitors? Just asking these questions makes the point. Virtually everything we do in this world today involves a substantial degree of uncertainty.

There is one industry that understands this kind of uncertainty well, and that views the issue of climate change with growing alarm. It is one of the world's largest—roughly the same size as the fossil-fuel industry. I am referring of course to the insurance industry, which insures many of the properties most vulnerable to climate change, and has suffered record damages in recent years. The general manager of Swiss Re, one of Europe's largest insurance companies, says, "There is a significant body of scientific evidence indicating that last year's record insured loss from natural catastrophes was not a random occurrence. . . . Failure to act would leave the insurance industry and its policyholders vulnerable to truly disastrous consequences."[10]

Note that Swiss Re and other insurers are not saying that climate change is certain. Rather, they are saying that as an uncertain trend with potentially disastrous consequences, climate change has many similarities with the other risks with which the insurance industry deals on a daily basis. When an insurance company decides to insure your house, it does not know whether or not the house is going to burn down. The kinds of principles used to evaluate risk and decide what premium to charge suggest a good analogy to the way society should be looking at global climate change.

Michaels is a lot less conservative than the average insurance executive. His argument is that we should throw out the precautionary principle, ignore the risk of climate change, and hope for the best. The bottom line is that Michaels has his own forecast, which happens to be at odds with most of the hundreds of climate scientists that are working on these issues. I simply ask you: Does it make sense to bet the planet on the optimistic assumptions of one contrarian? Indeed, a real conservative would argue that we should act now to slow the dangerous rise in greenhouse-gas emissions rather than risk having to reduce emissions drastically in the future, which really could disrupt the economy.

The Policy Options

In the same way that he has mischaracterized the science of climate change, so has Michaels distorted the policy options. The way he has framed the debate, I guess I would have to describe myself as being part of a "conspiracy" involving the vice-president of the United States, several hundred scientists around the world, and probably the Trilateral Commission as well. According to the Michaels theorem, we are all desperate to foster a government takeover of the economy —presumably in order to reduce everybody's wealth, revive Karl Marx, and so on.

Within the policy community there is actually a broad spectrum of views on how we ought to address the problem of climate change. Even within the environmental community, there are groups that favor carbon taxes, and others that favor regulation, or tradable permits. In other words, there is a range of opinions that do not necessarily correlate with how much alarm those holding the views feel about the problem itself. The majority opinion is that some sort of market mechanism is the most efficient way to reduce carbon dioxide emissions—for example, higher energy taxes that would be offset by a decline in labor and income taxes.

A grand governmental solution is not the way we are going to achieve the kind of energy system that is needed. I simply do not think that that is the pattern for successful innovation in any sector. Certainly there are government policies that can help spur efficient change, however. For example, the huge existing subsidies to coal and oil are clearly an impediment to the development of new renewable energy technologies. To spur private businesses and allow them to accelerate the move away from carbon-intensive energy systems, the key is to free up the energy markets, and get away from the public and private monopolies that control oil, gas, and electricity. We are beginning to see this happen in a number of countries, where innovative technologies have been fostered by such beneficial government policies. India and Germany, for example, are building numerous wind farms today.

In my opinion, reducing carbon emissions—even by the 60-80 per cent that will ultimately be required to stabilize carbon dioxide concentrations—will end up being a lot easier and less expensive than most economists and industry groups currently expect. In support of that argument, it is worth noting that there is a century-long trend of gradually lowering the carbon intensity of energy systems. When you learn that the Russian economy has five times the carbon intensity of the Japanese economy, you realize that the level of national carbon emissions is *inversely* related to economic success. Rising energy efficiency tends to reduce emissions, as does the broader trend from carbon-laden coal to progressively less carbon-intensive fuels such as oil, then to natural gas, and finally to renewable energy sources that emit no carbon. The many advanced electronic and materials technologies that have appeared in recent years provide opportunities to accelerate that trend. In fact, in 1994 we at the Worldwatch Institute published a book entitled *Power Surge: A Guide to the Coming Energy Revolution,* which makes the case for a gradual transition away from the kind of energy system we have today.[11]

Far from slowing global economic progress, the Framework Convention on Climate Change has the potential to accelerate it, by spurring countries to speed up investment in more energy-efficient infrastructure, to eliminate counterproductive energy subsidies, and to accelerate the development of new technologies. Already, in the two and a half years since the so-called Rio Treaty was signed, we have seen a dramatic acceleration in the development of renewable energy sources and natural gas in many parts of the world, while dependence on coal is being reduced in some nations. In many industrial and developing countries, the treaty has helped reform outdated domestic energy policies.

If it is implemented constructively—and aggressively—the Rio Treaty could turn out to be one of the best things that ever happened to the global economy. If the United States wants to be successful in the expanding energy markets of the next century, it will need to take a leading role in developing a sustainable energy system and stabilizing the earth's atmosphere. In that endeavor, ignoring the misguided words of Patrick Michaels would be a productive first step.

Comments

Patrick Michaels: The ozone issue is, I think, an absolutely false analogy of the global warming issue. As Christopher Flavin said, what actually happened with ozone was of greater magnitude than the models predicted. In climate change it's the opposite: you have a model that says something should be happening very rapidly and a planet that does not show that. Flavin then went on to say that climate is chaotic, that it changes suddenly. But outside of the polar regions, where climate changes rapidly for obvious reasons, I know of no long-term climate records that show any chaotic behavior.

Climatologists like to refer to climate as meta-stable. You do see large and rapid—from a geological perspective—changes in climate. We've had ice ages a few times. But deglaciation or glaciation doesn't occur overnight. These changes take a couple of hundred years. (A story went around that they occurred within ten years. That's scientifically untenable; you can't jiggle the energy equations enough to get that.)

Think about the kind of changes that accompanied the end of the last glaciation: in the high latitudes of the Northern Hemisphere you can see changes of plus or minus 5 degrees Celsius in mean temperature over approximately forty-year periods. That tells me two things. First, the earth's ecosystem, at least at those latitudes, is perfectly capable of dealing with that level of change. Where were the extinctions? Where are all the bodies? Second, what appears in the geologic record to be rapid change—and a couple of hundred years is rapid change geologically—from a human point of view is nothing. Two hundred years ago, technologically this society was *radically* different than it is today. If an ice age started to develop today, two hundred

---

Note: These participants are identified on pages 151-52.

years from now there wouldn't be much of a change. Two centuries of growing a glacier doesn't get you very much glacier. I can't believe that this society, given its information processing and technology, is going to fall apart over that time frame.

Richard Wright: I have been teaching environmental science for twenty-four years and am a co-author of one of the textbooks. I've been watching these issues as they have developed over time—looking at the science, reading the original articles—and have become convinced that global warming is a very real possibility. I'm perfectly willing to support policies right now that will reduce fossil-fuel use, for two reasons: one, because it will at least begin to move us in the right direction to prevent further global warming, and two, because other societal benefits would result, such as reducing pollution and reducing our dependence on Middle East oil. I think the consensus is very strongly in favor of, not the Global Circulation Models, but the physical realities behind them. The amount of warming that is going to happen is related to the concentration of greenhouse gases in the atmosphere, and we are adding CO_2 all the time. There's no end in sight. Why limit it to doubling? There could be three or four times as much CO_2 over the next hundred and fifty years, and if that happens, we're going to have a real disaster on our hands. So let's start trying to deal with it now.

Patrick Michaels: You have to understand the process of science to understand what scientific consensus means. Nature does not take a vote of scientists and proceed accordingly. If you ask people in the field, "What is the key piece of evidence that allows you to maintain this viewpoint?" everybody says the Vostok ice core. In this ice core, which goes back 150,000 years, there are changes in carbon dioxide and methane and changes in temperature. That to me is a remarkably *weak* argument, because the Vostok is a polar-region core. Climate in polar regions fluctuates dramatically and probably will fluctuate considerably with a change in the greenhouse gases; but it means very little, in all likelihood, for latitudes between 60° north and 60° south. So yes, we can say that the changes in the Vostok ice core are real, but this can't be used to determine the parameters of warming. The only thing you can do to parameterize warming is to look at the facts.

Richard Land: I want to put something on the table in the hope of challenging everyone to a paradigm shift. It seems to me that the kind of discussion we're having here is remarkably similar to the discussions we had during the decades prior to the collapse of the Soviet Union. What we were debating then was the arms race. How many times did we hear: How much defense is enough? How much deterrent is enough? People would say, "Surely this missile stockpile we have is enough," and the response would be, "Well, if it's not enough we'll wake up one morning in the smoldering ruins of what was once the United States and we'll say: Gosh, it wasn't enough." We had the same kinds of challenges to CIA projections that we have to scientists' projections. Obviously a lot of the CIA people were not neutral, nor was the defense industry neutral in building up the threat of a Soviet first strike against the United States. Once again, an imprecise science. What is the hard evidence? How many missiles do they have? Do they work? We now know that a lot of them probably wouldn't have worked; they probably wouldn't have cleared the silos. The argument was that if we are going to err, we need to err on the side of caution. "But we are spending all this money," said the critics. "Well," said the other side, "what's more important than defending the survival of our civilization?"

This might help to get us out of conservative/liberal mindset in which we tend to operate. Let's think about how some arguments used during the arms race can be applied to environmentalism. We know now that the CIA and the intelligence community overestimated the threat from the Soviet Union, that a good many Soviet missiles wouldn't have worked, that the Soviet Union in terms of its military and economic infrastructure was not a Second World country but a Third World country. Every time a CIA projection proved wrong, there was a loss of credibility to the defense and intelligence communities. I think that has clearly happened in my constituency over some of the wild projections of the doomsdayers among the environmentalists. The fact that some of the predictions have proved false has resulted in a loss of credibility that leads to less concern about the environment than there ought to be.

Another thing: a lot of us who took part in the arms-race debate now find ourselves with the shoe on the other foot in the environmental debate. For my part, if we were to err in the arms race, I wanted to err on the side of caution. But people who were conservative on the Cold War issue are those most likely to think that the environmentalists are overestimating the threat. There is also a correlation between environmentalists and those who thought that the Soviets were never a threat, that the threat was being manufactured to drive the military-industrial complex.

Christopher Flavin: I agree that there is an unfortunate tendency for people to line these issues up in an ideological framework that really doesn't work. Certainly there are some useful lessons to be gained from the mistakes of "conservatives" who overestimated Soviet military and economic strength in order to justify militarization of the U.S. economy. However, the current "debate" over climate change has important differences as well. For one thing, the warnings are not coming from "environmental doomsdayers" but from hundreds of leading scientists who publish their results in peer-reviewed scientific journals like *Nature* and *Science.* Unlike the CIA projections in the eighties, these assessments are not secret internal studies but are widely available to be scrutinized by hundreds of other scientists. Secondly, unlike the military situation in the eighties, we are not spending hundreds of billions of dollars to combat the threat of climate change. Rather, we are spending just a few billion dollars annually, most of it on essential scientific research. Given the scale of the climate threat, public *and* private spending on climate research and on climate-change prevention should be substantially *increased*.

Patrick Michaels: I think the Cold War analogy was very apt. I would answer it with a question: Were the CIA and the defense industry conspiring to create the consensus that the Soviet threat was large? They weren't conspiring. The reason for the belief was quite simple: it paid. In the matter of global warming, the environmental movement is a lot like the CIA in that it has an interest in keeping the issue alive, because it has been a very potent revenue-generator. When it became evident that the Soviet Union was going to crash internally, there were still voices on all the network discussion programs saying that the Soviets were still going to come and get us. It's a process called public choice. If the environmental issues didn't work that way, then there would be something wrong.

Fred Smith: In many ways the world is an ink blot, and we read into it evidence to support our own values, whether those values are individualistic or hierarchical or egalitarian. Jack Sommers at the University of North Carolina–Charlotte has suggested some basic questions to ask. Is something happening out there? (Were the Soviets building weapons? Is the earth warming?) Do we know why these things are occurring? (Why was the Soviet Union building up an army? Why is the earth warming?) Can we control the situation? Should we seek to arrest or to encourage the changes we are seeing? What are the offsetting advantages of change? (We know that greenhouse warming may have some positive effects, such as greater productivity of agriculture, deserts blooming into grasslands, a reduced likelihood of an ice age.) Finally, should intervention be private or political?

The "precautionary principle" says that when science and factual information are lacking or are not totally conclusive, we nonetheless should act—usually in the direction of slowing down technological and economic change, rather than encouraging it. The analogy of the precautionary principle is the old *Titanic* image. The world is a ship churning through unknown waters where there clearly are dangerous uncertainties such as icebergs. In that situation, doesn't it make sense to slow down? But if you were going to sail on that ship, would you want to weaken your ability to improve your sonar and radar capability? Would you want to cut down the horsepower of the engines? Would you want to reduce the wealth that would allow you to have more lifeboats on the ship? Wherever we are faced with uncertainty, the one thing we can do to protect ourselves against future dangers is to increase our capacities, our wealth, and our knowledge base so we are better able to address whatever disasters loom.

Craig Rucker: A question to Patrick Michaels: Are there in fact a growing number of scientists who are questioning whether global warming is occurring at all, or is it just a question of the pace at which it is happening?

Patrick Michaels: I believe it's the latter. You can't look at the Jones and Wigley temperature record and say that it doesn't show a warming of the surface temperature. The problem with that record is that so much of the warming took place before the greenhouse effect took off. Furthermore, those temperature departures that are shown across the Northern Hemisphere are departures from a 1951 to 1980 average.

Historically, the 1951-80 period is relatively cool. So the warming is being measured not from a hundred-year or even fifty-year average but from a thirty-year cool period.

Susan Drake: I have been working on these issues for ten years, through three administrations, for the State Department, EPA, the World Bank, Congress—all over the place in Washington. I'm wondering now how many scientists have been involved in the U.N.'s IPCC process. How many scientists from around the world have actually been investigating this and have come up with these conclusions that have pushed governments to take action against greenhouse warming?

Christopher Flavin: As part of the formal IPCC process? Probably 100 or 150.

Patrick Michaels: I would say roughly 250 participants, but about half of those are government functionaries who aren't scientists.

Susan Drake: In my experience, governments tend to be the last to move on issues. They don't tend to be the innovators or the progressive forces. The idea that on this particular issue, somehow governments have gotten ahead of science—particularly through the workings of the U.N., where everything operates at the level of the lowest common denominator—is quite amazing to me.

Ronald Bailey: At the Rio conference I was working as a reporter, going around and talking to people from the Third World. What they were looking at was what they hoped would be a huge pot of money. "Let's go with that climate-change treaty because we are going to get a lot of money out of those rich guys in the north." Governments can innovate quickly when it means they can grab power and money; they are not at all slow to expand. I used to be a government bureaucrat, too, for probably the world's most boring agency, the Federal Energy Regulatory Commission. It certainly did innovate quite rapidly when it needed to. For example, when gas made at garbage dumps was declared to be a manmade substance and in need of federal regulation —instantaneous response, no problem.

A great many environmentalists are saying, as Al Gore has done, that we must radically change our societies and our economies. They have a very high ethical hurdle to go over. They have to tell us, "Yes, the catastrophe that we predict is coming," before we respond in any drastic way. They have a moral obligation to persuade us, because they are asking us to make big changes in our whole way of life. I don't think they've met that challenge.

Richard Baer: I used to think I knew quite a bit about Buddhism, and the more I learned, the less convinced I was of knowing very much. I feel somewhat the same about global warming. A question for Patrick Michaels: If there were no substantial costs at all, do you, as a scientist, think it would make for a better future if we could level off or even decrease our production of CO_2?

Patrick Michaels: My preference as a scientist would be not to answer your question, because that's not my area. But it becomes my area when someone says that there is evidence that projection A will in fact occur and it will cost me and you money to deal with it. Then I have to say: Wait a minute, this projection doesn't seem to be borne out by the data. That's my bailiwick.

Richard Baer: If it turns out that really significant global warming should occur, are there emergency tactics we could take? Could we put enough dust or something else in the high atmosphere that would counteract it? Or are we really stuck if it does occur?

Patrick Michaels: We could probably reverse some of it. I don't think we could reverse 8 degrees of warming. It's very important to look at the data. Since sulfate aerosol emission is not a sufficient explanation for the lack of warming, enhancing some type of reflective emission is probably not going to counteract warming in large part. In some part, yes.

Fred Smith: When I was a kid in college and studying economics and political science, I remember the debate we faced at that time was over a painful choice America had to make. Many intellectuals at the time thought that the old capitalist system, with its private property and decentralized entrepreneurial activity, was interesting but inherently flawed. Far superior were the new centrally planned economies then emerging. The United States had to make a painful choice between the economic freedom of the past and economic efficiency in the future. The centrally planned economies would drive us into the dust unless we abandoned our nostalgia and went along with the new world.

That debate is now over. We know that there is no conflict between economic freedom and economic efficiency. We know that the only way to create wealth is to give people a stake in wealth creation. The people of the world are not going to get richer under government means. Now we have a similar debate over environmental issues. Are environmental policies best advanced collectively, or are they best advanced privately through creative voluntary arrangements? That debate is one-sided at the moment—in the environmental area today the reigning belief is that politics must do everything because we can't do it ourselves.

Making possible a private vision of environmental policy involves some tremendous challenges. But the ethical implications of giving our freedoms over to the political processes of the world are frightening. We should be talking ethics as much as science in this debate.

Christopher Flavin: It seems to me that the points Fred Smith is touching on are important ones, though he has badly mischaracterized the kind of environmental policies that are called for by the climate convention. Perhaps we can get closer to consensus on the policy issues than on the scientific ones. The government is of course already heavily involved in the energy sector today, with mainly negative results—subsidizing the most environmentally damaging energy sources, often at the behest of powerful industries.

I do not think it is either necessary or desirable to have massive governmental investment in the technologies for a low-carbon economy. But government policies will need to be reformed. For much of this century we were building up a fossil-fuel economy, and we developed various subsidies that benefited not just the coal and oil industries but also the railroad and other related industries that supported that infrastructure. Those subsidies are still in place today. So I think the key really is to accelerate technological change and to allow private capital to work more aggressively in bringing these new technologies into the market. In most countries, that will require changing government policies, reducing subsidies, opening up monopolistic utilities and other energy systems. That is something that virtually all of us can support.

Ron Sider: I find it distressing that we have not been able to get beyond enormous disagreements on the scientific data so we can deal with the ethical questions. Is there no way to design some structures for reviewing the scientific data together where people who disagree really *listen* to one other?

Patrick Michaels: In October 1994 I participated in a meeting in Washington that had to do with a letter from a congressman about the validity of climate models. Some remarkable things happened at that meeting. All of a sudden the climate modelers who were there —and they were the same people who ran the model that I said earlier is performing so badly—agreed to my point about sulfates and several other points that are too technical for this discussion. In other words, all of a sudden I was part of the consensus.

Let me tell you why this happened and make a prediction about the future. When the Rio Treaty went into effect six months after the fiftieth signatory approved, all of a sudden the budget for climate modeling was cut. The quarry had been shot, and now there was no reason for the hunting party to be as funded as it had been. The climate-modeling community was horrified. Now, all of a sudden, those who have brought up internally consistent data-based arguments are consensual, because, you see, it serves that community; that's the way science works. Now we in fact can bring this person up here and say: Yes, there are problems with our models; please reinstate our funding. This is exactly what happened in NAPAP, the acid-rain assessment project. We produced a comprehensive report, and as soon as it came out, funding for the research dropped, even though the report itself was much more equivocal.

Given this pattern and the 1994 change in Congress, I predict that the consensus on global warming over the next two years will shift. It will shift towards an admission of less warming in the future and less disastrous effects and increased uncertainty. This will not happen because the science changed, but because those who hold the hearings and develop the consensus have changed.

Ron Sider: If political changes lead people to change their scientific conclusions, then we are in trouble.

Patrick Michaels: We are in the real world.

3

Here Comes the Sun

Gregg Easterbrook

Few ideas are more deeply entrenched in our political culture than that of impending ecological doom. Beginning in 1962, when Rachel Carson warned readers of *The New Yorker* that pollution was a threat to all human and animal life on the planet, pessimistic appraisals of the health of the environment have been issued with increasing urgency. And yet, thanks in large part to her warnings, a powerful political movement was born—its coming-out party, the first Earth Day demonstration, took place on April 22, 1970—and a series of landmark environmental bills became law: the Clean Air Act (1970), the Clean Water Act (1972), and the Endangered Species Act (1973). These laws and their equivalents in Western Europe, along with a vast array of private efforts spurred by the environmental consciousness that Carson helped raise, have been a stunning success. In both the United States and Europe, environmental trends are, for the most part, positive; and environmental regulations, far from being burdensome and expensive, have proved to be strikingly effective, have cost less than was anticipated, and have made the economies of the countries that have put them into effect stronger, not weaker.

Gregg Easterbrook is the author of *A Moment on the Earth: The Coming Age of Environmental Optimism* (Viking, 1995). This essay, based on material in that book, first appeared in the April 10, 1995, issue of *The New Yorker* (©1995 by the author) and is used here by permission in a slightly abridged form.

Nevertheless, the vocabulary of environmentalism has continued to be dominated by images of futility, crisis, and decline. In 1988, Thomas Berry, an essayist popular among ecologists, wrote that "the planet cannot long endure present modes of human exploitation." In 1990, Gaylord Nelson, the former senator from Wisconsin, who was a prime mover behind the first Earth Day, said that environmental problems "are a greater threat to Earth's life-sustaining systems than a nuclear war." And in 1993 Vice President Al Gore said that the planet now was suffering "grave and perhaps irreparable damage." But, at least insofar as the Western world in concerned, this line of thought is an anachronism, rendered obsolete by its own success.

Environmentalists are not the only people reluctant to acknowledge the good news. Advocates at both ends of the political spectrum, each side for its own reasons, seem to have tacitly agreed to play it down. The left is afraid of the environmental good news because it undercuts stylish pessimism; the right is afraid of the good news because it shows that government regulations might occasionally amount to something other than wickedness incarnate, and actually produce benefits at an affordable cost.

This is a bad bargain, for liberals especially. Their philosophy is under siege on many fronts—crime, welfare, medical care, and education, among others. So why not trumpet the astonishing, and continuing, record of success in environmental protection?

The Achievements

Consider some of what has been accomplished in this country in the quarter century since the first Earth Day. Thanks to legislation, technical advances, and lawsuits that have forced polluters to pay liability costs, America's air and water are getting cleaner, forests are expanding, and many other environmental indicators are on the upswing.

Smog has declined by about a third, though there are now 85 per cent more vehicles being driven 105 per cent more miles a year. In Los Angeles, the decline has been particularly dramatic: smog has decreased by almost 50 per cent, during a time when the city's vehicle population has risen 65 per cent. Since 1970, airborne levels of lead have declined 98 per cent nationwide; annual emissions of carbon monoxide are down 24 per cent; emissions of sulfur dioxide, the chief cause of acid rain, have fallen 30 per cent, even as the use of coal, the main source of sulfur, has almost doubled; and emissions of fine soot, which causes respiratory disease, have fallen 78 per cent. Air-quality trends are sufficiently positive that several urban areas, such as Detroit and Kansas City, have been removed from the federal smog-watch list, and none have been added.

Signs of improved water quality are equally in evidence. In 1972, only a third of the bodies of water in the United States were safe for fishing and swimming. Today, almost two-thirds are safe, and the proportion continues to rise. Excessive phosphorus, a barometer of pollution, peaked in the Great Lakes around fifteen years ago; readings now are between 40 and 70 per cent lower. Boston Harbor, Chesapeake Bay, Long Island Sound, Puget Sound, and other bodies of water that were once on the verge of biological death are showing steady improvement.

Another sign of progress is the decline of toxic hazards. Quarrels over the final disposition of old chemical-waste dumps continue to bedevil courts and politicians, but, because of tight regulations and industrial liability, the creation of new toxic dumps has nearly stopped, and is unlikely ever to resume. One of the largest chemical-waste sites, the Rocky Mountain Arsenal, near Denver, where nerve gases, pesticides, and firebombs were once manufactured, used to be described as the deadliest place on earth. In 1992, it was designated a National Wildlife Refuge; a number of rare species now thrive there. Their presence hardly proves that chemical wastes are somehow good for birds and animals, of course, but it does show that toxic wastes can be and are being contained. Just between 1988 and 1992, American industry's toxic emissions fell 35 per cent, even as petrochemical production expanded. Thanks to tight regulation of the dangerous compound dioxin, an estimated thirty pounds of this substance will be emitted in 1995 by all known United States sources combined, which suggests that the problem is almost certainly under control.

In recent years, several worrisome environmental trends have either declined from their peak or ended altogether. The amount of household trash dumped in landfills, for example, has been diminishing since the late 1980s, when recycling began to take hold. Recycling, which was a fringe idea a decade ago, is now a major growth industry, and is converting more than 20 per cent of America's municipal wastes into useful products. Despite start-up problems, many municipal recycling programs now pay for themselves. Emissions of chlorofluorocarbons, which deplete the ozone layer, have been declining since 1987. Studies now suggest that ozone-layer replenishment may begin within a decade. Dozens of American cities once dumped raw sludge into the ocean. This category of pollution passed into history in 1992, when the final load of New York City sludge slithered off a barge imaginatively named Spring Brook. Today, instead of being dumped into the ocean, municipal sludge is either disposed of in regulated landfills or, increasingly, put to good use as fertilizer.

It may be hard to believe, but efficient new manufacturing techniques, recycling, and other technological advances are allowing us to consume some natural resources at lower rates. Eric Larson, of Princeton University, and his colleagues have shown that American per capita use of ammonia, cement (limestone and clay), aluminum, chlorine, and steel has been flat or falling for a decade or more.

Even though Americans use more paper than they did a decade ago, this country is increasingly covered by a canopy of trees. It is commonly assumed that America is undergoing deforestation, but reforestation has been the trend for at least half a century. Everyone knows that in some parts of the United States urban acreage is expanding; what is much less widely recognized is that, in some areas, forest acreage is expanding rapidly, too. (For example, in the mid-1800s about a third of Massachusetts was wooded; today, though the state has six times the population, three-fifths of its area is forestland.) High-yield agriculture allows farmers to produce more food from the same or less land, and much of the acreage that is withdrawn from agriculture ends up reverting to woodland or prairie. The supposed crisis of the vanishing American farm, which has been regularly bemoaned throughout the post-war ear, has in fact been a blessing to nature. And acid rain has proved less damaging to trees than was once projected, and is in decline. At the same time, the acreage of America held in preservation has risen steadily through this century and now amounts to more than two times the area of California. In 1994 alone, 7.4 million acres of ancient forest in the Pacific Northwest were put into reserves by President Clinton, and nearly ten million acres of Southwestern desert were declared off limits by Congress—a combined area larger than the state of West Virginia.

America's record of protecting species threatened with extinction, which is often depicted as dismal, is in truth enviable. Since 1973, when the Endangered Species Act took effect, seven animal species in North America have disappeared, but several hundred others once considered certain to die out continue to exist in the wild. A number of species, including the bald eagle and the Arctic peregrine falcon, are doing so well that they have been or are being taken off the priority-protection list.

The Bottom Line

Even more extraordinary than America's environmental progress of the past generation is the fact that these advances have been achieved in affordable and practical ways. When pollution controls for cars were first proposed, in 1970, automakers predicted that the required systems would cost about $3,000 per car in today's dollars. Instead, controls now add between $500 and $1,000 to the price of a new vehicle, and they work amazingly well: current models emit an average of 80 per cent less pollution per mile than was emitted by new cars in 1970. Moreover, fuel-efficiency gains have reduced the typical car's annual gasoline consumption by around three hundred gallons. The fuel savings offset the equipment costs, with the result that for motorists the environmental features on new cars are essentially free of charge.

This is not an isolated example. In 1990, when new acid-rain controls were imposed on power plants, they were expected to cost about $750 per ton of pollution avoided; instead, the price today is $150 per ton. Monsanto, the chemical and pharmaceutical giant, has been able to cut toxic air emissions by 90 per cent without excessive expense, at least in part because savings from the recycling of chemicals have offset the costs of pollution-reduction technology. The installation of high-efficiency commercial lighting systems—inspired in part by the 1990 version of the Clean Air Act—is saving business tens of millions of dollars a year in expenses.

Solar power and wind power, disappointments in the past, appear to be on the verge of a takeoff. In late 1994, the energy conglomerate Enron announced plans to break ground in Nevada for the first unsubsidized, commercial-scale solar-electric array. The array will be built for profit, at a cost competitive with that of fossil-fueled generators. Though fossil fuels today seem indispensable, they may be supplanted by renewable energy sources in the near future. Today, the energy economy of the Western world is closer to operation on a renewable-power basis than it was a century ago to operation on the basis of the headlong combustion of petroleum. Should fossil-fuel use wane, in historic terms, as quickly as it arose, the greenhouse problem could almost solve itself.

It's true, of course, that some environmental programs are muddled. For instance, the Endangered Species Act can have the unfair effect of penalizing landholders who discover rare creatures on their property, by prohibiting use of the land. In the main, though, conservation has been an excellent investment for society. Environmental initiatives worked well even in their early years, when they were driven by top-heavy federal edicts. They work even better as new regulations have centered on market mechanisms and voluntary choice; new acid-rain reductions, for example, are being achieved at unexpectedly affordable rates, thanks to a free-market program under which companies trade pollution "allowances" with one another. Western market economies excel at producing what they are asked to produce, and, increasingly, the market is being asked to produce conservation. Environmental reform should be seen as a boon to Western industry, impelling it toward efficiencies that enhance its long-term competitiveness; indeed, environmentalism may be saving the consumer society from itself.

The unmistakable trend toward environmental progress in the West should not delude us into supposing that from now on the global environment will somehow take care of itself. Throughout much of the Third World, basic water sanitation is awful, the air is thick with pollutants, and wildlife loss is rampant. Nor can we afford to be complacent about the domestic environment. Though most indicators in the West are positive, danger signs nevertheless remain, including the decline of the Pacific salmon and the unresolved problem of how to deal with the nuclear detritus of the Cold War. The bewildering array of environmental statutes in the Western world (there are sixteen major laws in the United States alone) needs to be streamlined with a simplified general conservation law that would focus on habitat preservation, for this is likely to be the primary ecological issue of the coming century.

The Naysayers

Environmentalism has become a core American political value, close to unassailable even among conservatives. A recent Times Mirror survey is typical. A majority of the respondents agreed with the statement that "government regulation of business usually does more harm than good," yet 78 per cent of the same respondents also think that "this country should do whatever it takes to protect the environment."

The ecological recovery in progress in the West has many heroes: pioneers such as Rachel Carson; environmental activists who carried on the fight; scientists and engineers who have increasingly made clean technology viable; even some business leaders who have become converts to conservation. Political liberalism, which provided the legislative muscle, deserves a large share of the credit, too. Yet liberalism resists the glad tidings of ecological rebound. When liberal intellectuals and Democratic politicians talk about nature in the vocabulary of fashionable defeatism, they sell themselves and their philosophies short.

A telling example of liberal discomfort with environmental optimism came in the 1988 Presidential campaign. Candidate George Bush began his comeback from a deep deficit in the polls with a memorable TV commercial that pronounced the waters of Boston Harbor the dirtiest in America, and pinned the blame on his opponent, Governor Michael Dukakis. After the commercial ran, Dukakis was silent about the harbor, seeming to accede to the charge. Many analysts consider the Boston Harbor spot to have been the turning point in the 1988 campaign. Yet the commercial was shot so as to frame out of the picture a four-billion-dollar complex rising in the background —the largest water-treatment system in United States history. Its construction had already begun, at regional expense. At the time Bush made his commercial, there was every reason to hope that the new system would clean Boston Harbor rapidly; it has, and the harbor is now safe again for swimming. So why didn't Dukakis respond to Bush immediately by pointing out that a solution was at hand? Because doing so would have required Dukakis to talk about the environment in upbeat tones.

More recently, Carol Browner, the current head of the Environmental Protection Agency, fell victim to the same syndrome. In 1994, Browner, a lifelong liberal Democrat, gave a series of speeches pointing out that there were many signs of environmental progress. She proposed a "common-sense initiative" and revisions that would improve conservation law by adding cost-benefit analysis, simplifying rules for cleanups, and eliminating regulatory overkill. And she did this long before anyone had heard the words "Contract with America." In 1994, Browner's hopeful declarations sank without a trace into the abyss of conventional opinion. Her effort fizzled because Democrats, then still in control of Congress, were put off by the suggestion of environmental good news, and also because White House support was faint.

Liberalism is on the defensive today because, as a philosophy, it concentrates almost entirely on what has failed—about America, about public policy, about daily life. Obviously, there are failures aplenty, but there are successes as well. In the West, environmental protection is the leading post-war triumph of progressive government. Because of this, the notion of impending doomsday is about to expire. We are about to become environmental optimists.

A Response

Ronald Bailey

Gregg Easterbrook has largely got the data right on environmental trends, but he is way off the mark as to why the trends are so positive. Why? Because he confuses the results of economic progress and wealth creation with the effects of environmental regulation. He fails to understand that the affluence created by free markets precedes and enables environmental cleanup. Merely imposing government regulations simply doesn't work without the economic wherewithal to implement them. In fact, regulations can have pernicious effects on the environment.

As Department of Interior analyst Indur Goklany argues, "anything which retards economic growth also retards ultimate environmental cleanup." Goklany shows that for most pollutants there is a threshold of wealth at which the amount of a pollutant begins to decline, and he calls that threshold the "environmental transition." For example, particulates like smoke and soot peak when average per capita incomes reach $3,200, while sulfur dioxide peaks at $3,700. Because of the importance of safe drinking water, fecal coliform bacteria in rivers peaks at the much lower income level of $1,400. Imposing expensive American-style command-and-control environmental regulations on

---

Ronald Bailey is the editor of *The True State of the Planet* (Free Press, 1995), producer of the national weekly public television series "Think Tank," and the author of *Eco-Scam: The False Prophets of Ecological Apocalypse.* This response is excerpted from a review entitled "Earth to Easterbrook" that appeared in the May 29, 1995, issue of *National Review* (©1995 by National Review, Inc.) and is reprinted by permission.

poor countries could easily end up delaying environmental improvements in those countries by slowing their economic growth.

Easterbrook celebrates environmental regulation as a shining success of contemporary liberalism. But we now can see just how costly the clumsy top-down environmental regulations he celebrates are becoming. Most of the big, obvious problems, like the dumping of raw sewage into rivers, have been dealt with, and now we are at the point of diminishing or even negative returns. The 1970 Clean Air Act cost about $6 billion annually to implement but created about $36 billion in health and environmental benefits. By contrast, the 1990 Clean Air Act amendments cost about $35 billion annually to implement and provide only about $10 billion in benefits.

In his book, *A Moment on the Earth,* Easterbrook also wrongheadedly advocates the "precautionary principle." Even though he shows that the evidence for a catastrophic global warming is practically nonexistent, he nevertheless urges that the world's economy begin shifting away from fossil fuels to other more expensive (and speculative) technologies and energy sources. In the case of global warming, the "precautionary principle" says we should cut fossil-fuel use just because we don't know all the consequences that burning fossil fuels will have.

Easterbrook and the environmentalists fail to recognize that following the precautionary principle can lead to greater environmental degradation. But moving forward using intelligent trial and error uncovers new knowledge and increases resources and wealth, and greater knowledge and wealth give human communities resilience, enabling them to respond flexibly and effectively to the unexpected. This is why just fourteen Americans died when Hurricane Andrew hit Florida and Louisiana in 1992, whereas impoverished people in Bangladesh die by the thousands when cyclones strike their villages. Better roads, housing, medical facilities, and emergency response measures made possible by American wealth make it far easier to weather storms in Florida than in Bangladesh.

Easterbrook's call, in his book, for handing over more of the environment and the economy to political management is even more perplexing when you consider his harsh criticism of bungling by agencies like the Bureau of Land Management and the Forest Service. He even quotes a former Environmental Protection Agency staffer who says, "Everything the EPA does is driven by political considerations rather than scientific considerations. The science is always tailored to support whatever has already been concluded politically." Conservatives have known this for a long time.

Easterbrook has done a good job of cataloguing the environmental good news, thereby helping to undercut the alarmism that has driven so much government regulation of the environment. Environmentalists understand that only an unrelenting drumbeat of doom will keep the public crying for more regulation, and they will not appreciate Easterbrook's efforts to dissipate the gloom. But as what he calls the "coming age of environmental optimism" dawns, the policies he praises will be increasingly seen as inefficient and harmful.

4

The Challenge of Biocentrism

Thomas Sieger Derr

At first glance I might appear to be an unlikely person to be critical of the environmental movement in any way. A sometime countryman, I usually know where the wind is and what phase of the moon we're in. I take good care of my small woodland, and I love my dogs. My personal predilections carry over into public policy, too. I champion the goals of reducing the waste stream, improving air and water quality, preserving the forests, protecting wildlife. I think of environmentalism as in some form a necessary and inevitable movement.

But by current standards that does not make me much of an environmentalist, for I am profoundly unhappy with the direction of current environmental philosophy, and most especially because I am a Christian. My trouble stems partly from the determination of mainstream environmentalism to blame Christianity for whatever ecological trouble we are in. This is a piece of historical nonsense that apparently thrives on repetition, so that every time it appears in print more people feel free to quote the source as authoritative, and each reference has a further multiplier effect.

Although a canard of this sort cannot surely be traced to a single

---

Thomas Sieger Derr is chair of the Department of Religion and Biblical Literature at Smith College, Northampton, Massachusetts. He is the author of *Ecology and Human Need* (Westminster, 1975) and of many essays on religion and ecology.

source, probably the closest we can come to its origin is an essay by the late, formidable medieval historian Lynn White, Jr., called "The Historical Roots of Our Ecologic Crisis," which appeared in *Science* in 1967 and has since enjoyed virtually eternal life in anthologies.[1] It is cited as evidence of the need for an alternative religion, as for example by George Sessions, premier philosopher of the currently popular "Deep Ecology" movement: "The environmental crisis [is] fundamentally a crisis of the West's anthropocentric philosophical and religious orientations and values."[2]

It is not so much that White himself blamed Christianity; he was far too careful a historian for that, and he wrote, moreover, as a Christian and an active churchman. But his essay was used by others to promote darker purposes.

To be sure, White gave them ammunition. He traced the modern technological exploitation of nature back through the ages to the famous "dominion" passage in Genesis 1:28, which gives humanity some form of supremacy over the rest of creation. Because, he argued, technology is now ecologically "out of control," it is fair to say that "Christianity bears a huge burden of guilt" for this result. We need to reject "the Christian axiom that nature has no reason for existence save to serve man." We must overcome our "orthodox Christian arrogance toward nature." White even gave his blessing to the counterculture's espousal of alternative religions: "More science and more technology are not going to get us out of the present ecologic crisis until we find a new religion, or rethink our old one. . . . The hippies . . . show a sound instinct in their affinity for Zen Buddhism and Hinduism, which conceive the man-nature relationship as very nearly the mirror image of the Christian view."

Is Christianity really the ecological culprit? And did White really say that it is? The answer to both questions is no.

Many scholars have concluded that Christianity made an important contribution to the rise of science and technology in the West, but to make it the only cause would be too much. Yes, the doctrine of creation separates nature from God, makes it not itself divine, and suggests strongly that inquiry into its workings is a pious study of the mind of the Maker. That way of looking at the world surely abets the scientific and technological culture. But it is not a *sufficient* condition for the appearance of that culture, which did not arise in lands dominated by Eastern Christianity but only in the Latin West, and then only after a millennium. Nor is it a *necessary* condition, for science flourished without benefit of Christianity in China, ancient Greece, and the medieval Islamic world.

Neither can we say that it is chiefly Christian lands that are environmentally heedless. Ecological destruction like overgrazing and deforestation, sometimes enough to cause the fall of civilizations, has been committed by Egyptians, Persians, Romans, Aztecs, Indians, and even Buddhists. This probably comes as a surprise to no one except those gullible Westerners who romanticize other cultures of which they know very little. There is, for example, a noted Western ecologist who, despising his own civilization, extols "the Eastern and gentle Pacific cultures in which man lives (or lived) a leisurely life of harmony with nature."[3] That could only have been written by someone who knows nothing of the sorry, violent history of those peoples.

What, then, does produce the technological society? And what causes ecological pillage? As to technology, we may guess at primitive origins in simple artisanship and the domestication of animals; the natural human quest for labor-saving devices; trade and commerce with other societies where these developments are further advanced; or just the natural momentum of technological change, once started in however small a way. Other likely suspects include geography, climate, population growth, urbanism, and democracy. To this mix add the idea that the world is an intelligible order ruled by general principles, which we received from the ancient Greeks, mediated powerfully (as A. N. Whitehead asserted[4]) by the medieval insistence on the rationality of God; or perhaps the rise of purely *secular* philosophy celebrating human mastery over nature, as in Bacon, Descartes, and Leibnitz. That is quite a list. Given this wealth of candidates, it would be impossible to sort out what the primary influences really are, and even White acknowledged that the causes are finally mysterious.

As for the causes of ecological harm, we may cite first the simple fact that there are more people on the earth than ever before, and their search for food and shelter frequently assaults the world around them. It is, notably, not only the factories of the developed nations, but the daily gathering and burning of wood for fuel by rural people in the Third World, along with the depredations of their domestic animals, that have damaged the world's soils and dirtied its air (which in the Third World is far more polluted than ours). Of course industrial development has caused ecological damage, but much of that is the result of ignorance and error, mistakes often quite correctable. Noisy voices in the environmental movement attribute the damage to corporate greed, and the more fanciful among them go searching for deeper roots in capitalist culture, which in turn they find spawned by Christian theology in some form. It is simpler and surely more accurate to say that human self-seeking is a constant in our natures that no culture, no matter what its religion, has managed to eliminate.

Lynn White really did not blame Christianity for our environmental difficulties. By "orthodox Christian arrogance toward nature" he did *not* mean, he later said, that arrogance toward nature is orthodox Christian doctrine, only that presumably orthodox Christians have been arrogant toward nature. By "the Christian axiom that nature has no reason for existence save to serve man" he meant, he claimed, that some Christians have *regarded* it as an axiom, not that it is a matter of true faith.[5] Qualifications like these really vitiate the apparent argument in his "Historical Roots" essay, which was that Christians were heedless of nature *because* they were Christians. But on reflection, after absorbing the storm, White retreated to saying only that Christians, like human beings everywhere, found it possible to misappropriate certain elements from their religious tradition to serve their selfish ends.

Having talked with White at some length about his essay, I believe that, although he may have been pleased at the notice it received, he was also disturbed at the way it was used. He was only half joking when he wrote me about the "theology of ecology," saying, "Of course, I claim to be the founder!" But surely he would disown many of his offspring.

The Christian Approach to Nature

What is the *real* orthodox Christian attitude toward nature? It is, in a word, stewardship. We are trustees for that which does not belong to us. "The earth is the Lord's, and the fullness thereof; the world and they that dwell therein" (Ps. 24:1). The implications of this idea for environmentalism are profound and, I think, wholly positive. They have been spelled out in different ways by many writers, including Douglas John Hall in *The Steward,* Loren Wilkinson and his colleagues in *Earthkeeping in the Nineties,* and my own book of twenty years ago, *Ecology and Human Need.*[6]

The rough historical evidence suggests that this theoretical obligation has not been without its practical results. For example, some Christian lands in Europe have been farmed in an ecologically stable manner for centuries. Rene Dubos says flatly, "The Judeo-Christian peoples were probably the first to develop on a large scale a pervasive concern for land management and an ethic of nature."[7] Clarence Glacken, one of the most patient and exhaustive historians of these matters, concludes from his survey of the vast literature, "I am convinced that modern ecological theory . . . owes its origin to the design argument," the idea so prominent in Christian theology of all ages that the complexity of the world is the work of a creator God.[8] Lynn White knew this, too. And in the past it has been common for even the ecological critics of Christianity to say that the Christians' problem is only that they did not take their own doctrines seriously enough.

What is new in our world today is a rejection of this semi- or pseudo-irenic view and its replacement by a root-and-branch attack on the doctrine of stewardship itself by that increasingly powerful and pervasive school of environmental thought known as biocentrism. There are many variations of biocentrism, of course, and one must be careful not to overgeneralize. But it is fair to say of nearly all varieties that they find the idea of stewardship repulsively anthropocentric, implying as it plainly does that human beings are in charge of nature, meant to manage it for purposes that they alone are able to perceive. Stewardship, says Richard Sylvan (ex-Routley), means "Man as tyrant."[9] May we think of ourselves as the earth's gardeners? Bad metaphor: gardening is controlling the earth's fecundity in a way that nature, left to its own devices, would not do. Human design is wrongly imposed.

The problem is simply compounded by Christian theism, which places human beings at the apex of nature by design of the ultimate giver of life. Made, as we say, in the image of God, we give ourselves license to claim that our interests as a species take precedence over those of the rest of creation; stewardship of the creation means mainly that we should manage it so that it sustains us indefinitely. Nature is made for us, as we are made for God. Here, say the biocentrists, is the bitter harvest of anthropocentrism: human selfishness, parochialism, chauvinism, "speciesism" (the awful term Peter Singer uses of those who reject animal rights), moral naïveté, a profanation of nature, self-importance and pride carried to their extreme. Regarding humankind as of more inherent worth than other species is, says Paul Taylor, like regarding noblemen of more inherent worth than peasants. A claim to human superiority is "a deep-seated prejudice, . . . a wholly arbitrary claim . . . an irrational bias in our own favor."[10] Lynn White was right after all: it is simply arrogance.

Rights in Nature

What do the biocentrists propose instead? Their most fundamental proposition is that nature itself, the life process as a whole, is the primary locus of value. Within that process all species have value, intrinsic value, just because they *are,* because they would not *be* if they did not have an appropriate niche in the ecology of the whole. And if they have intrinsic value, we must say that they have rights of some sort, claims on us for appropriate treatment, an integrity of their own that is not available for our mere willful disposition.

Notice that the alleged rights of non-human entities do not depend on their possession of any attributes, like rationality or language or even sentience. That would be subtle anthropocentrism, say the biocentrists. It would make a semblance to human characteristics the test of value—a mistake made by many of the animal-rights advocates and one that separates them from the biocentrists. We must say instead that all entities have value simply in themselves. They have their own purposes, or "good," which they value, either consciously or unconsciously. Their value, and their consequent rights, depend solely on their essential need to be themselves, on their own "vital interests."[11]

This is, incidentally, the way a biocentrist would dispose of the animal-rights argument that human infants or mentally defective human beings may be surpassed by animals in certain qualities, such as intelligence or adaptability, and yet we would not (or most of us would not) deny human rights to these human beings; so why not give animals rights? The answer, says the biocentrist—and here, for once, I would agree—is that rights inhere in a class or species, and not in the possession of certain qualities that individuals in that species possess. My difference, as I will make plain in a moment, is that I would not extend rights below the human level.[12]

Intrinsic Value in Nature

Since the assertion that the natural world has rights we must honor begins with the claim that the natural world has intrinsic value, let us spend a moment on this prior claim. No one, to my knowledge, has worked harder or with greater care to establish this idea—that natural entities have value independent of human beings (or, for that matter, independent of God, whom he does not mention)—than Holmes Rolston.[13] If, as I will claim, even *his* most careful and gracefully expressed formulations cannot stand, then one may suppose the biocentrists' foundations generally are weak.

To Rolston, the ability to support life is a natural good that the earth possesses without us, which means that the human experience of satisfaction is not necessary to have a "good." The earth is able to produce value without us. We recognize the presence of that objective value when we value our natural science, "for no study of a worthless thing can be intrinsically valuable."[14] Organisms are living beings and hence have a good for themselves, maintaining their own life; and this good is a value that can claim our respect. In fact, "the living individual . . . is per se an intrinsic value."[15]

Rolston admits that the human participant supplies value to an object: "No value can in principle . . . be altogether independent of a valuing consciousness. . . . If all consciousness were annihilated at a stroke, there would be no good or evil, . . . no right or wrong; only impassive phenomena would remain." However, "to say that something is valuable means that it is able to be valued, if and when human valuers come along, but it has this property whether or not humans . . . ever arrive." The value is already in the thing, hence "intrinsic." Rolston does not like any account of value in natural things that depends on human psychology. He wants the value to emerge from nature directly, so that we can value the object "for what it is in itself." Value may increase with the attention of human beings, but it is present without them. Thus his theory is "biocentric."[16]

On the contrary, I argue that, with the important theistic exception noted below, we human beings *supply* the value, that nature is valuable because we find it so. There is no value without a valuer. Values are for someone or some thing. A thing can provide value to someone, and in that sense it possesses value, i.e., the capacity to provide value for someone. That is not the same as "intrinsic" value, which is value in and for the thing itself, whatever anyone makes of it. The mere fact that we value studying a particular thing does not make that thing intrinsically valuable; it makes it valuable *for us.* Someone may find it valuable for his peace of mind to finger worry beads, but that does not mean that we must accord those beads intrinsic value. Some elderly recluses have been known to save newspapers for years, valuing the accumulating mountain highly. But that does not make these old papers *intrinsically* valuable. Mosquitos or bacteria may have a goal or drive for themselves in perpetuating their life; but that is quite different from having an *intrinsic* value that other, conscious beings are required to acknowledge.

The attempt of Rolston and other biocentrists—J. Baird Callicott, for example—to distinguish between human appreciation of nature's intrinsic value, and the value that human beings add to nature by appreciating it, strikes me as hairsplitting. It is much more compelling and credible to say simply that a natural object may generate value for us not by itself but only in conjunction with our situation. We supply the value; the object contributes its being. Value is not a term appropriate to it in isolation, by itself.

The Amorality of Nature

The discussion of value takes a different course if we are theists who accept the doctrine of creation as the foundation of our environmental philosophy, or theology. We may rightly say, as James Nash does, that all creatures must reflect their Maker in some way, and that a presumption of value in their favor is not unreasonable.[17] This is not to say that natural entities have intrinsic value; their value still depends on the valuer. But here the valuer is other than human beings. God bestows the value, which still does not belong to the object as such.

This is a well-developed idea with impeccable Thomist credentials; yet it does not solve our ecological problem. If anything, it makes the problem more difficult. To say that "God saw everything that he had made, and behold, it was very good" establishes well our obligation to respect the natural world; it is the foundation of our stewardship duty, of course. But we still face, and in a peculiarly painful form (for it raises the ancient problem of theodicy), the observable amorality of nature and its frequent hostility to us. That nature is full of what we perceive as violence and ugliness is beyond dispute. It is the realm of the food chain, of brute struggle and painful death. Surprisingly, no one has put it more candidly and vividly than Rolston himself:

> Wildness is a gigantic food pyramid, and this sets value in a grim, deathbound jungle. Earth is a slaughterhouse, with life a miasma rising over the stench. Nothing is done for the benefit of another. . . . Blind and ever urgent exploitation is nature's driving theme.[18]

Worse yet, from our point of view, nature is frequently hostile to our human lives. From violent storm to volcanic eruption to drought to killer viruses, to say nothing of the cosmic possibilities that could end our lives in one great, sudden bang, the natural world is certainly not unambiguously our friend.

Can one read an ethic out of this natural behavior? Not likely, or at least not an ethic that any Christian could for a moment tolerate. It is not that nature is immoral, for to say that would be to read our human values into this world. But nature is certainly amoral, and we would not begin to derive our ethical standards from its actions. Nevertheless the biocentrists, bound to locate value primarily in this amoral world, find something to cherish there, something that rises above the brutality of the food chain, something that relativizes the ugliness. Some choose the harmony that they profess to see behind the apparent chaos, the patterns that repeat themselves, the balances that are restored. Other biocentrists admire nature's vitality, fecundity, and regenerative power, its strength, endurance, and dynamism, even in the midst of its fury. New life emerges from rotting carcasses and burned forests. "Ugliness," says Rolston, "though present at time in particulars, is not the last word. . . . Over time nature will bring beauty out of this ugliness."[19]

But seeing it that way is a matter of choice. Harmony in an ecosystem is only apparent, superficial. There are emergent forces that triumph, species that disappear, balances that are permanently upset. To see harmony is to look selectively. Harmony, like beauty, is mostly in the eye of the beholder. If it is natural power and regenerative strength that enthrall us, we can love the rapid reproduction of cancer cells, or the terrible beauty of a tornado. We can love what kills us. Over time, nature means to destroy this world. The death of our sun might be beautiful if there were anyone to see it, I suppose, even though it would mark the end of planet earth. We can appreciate the natural facts any way we choose. To say it once again: we supply the value.

But what shall we say to those theists who reply that surely God must value what he has made? Can we discern what God intends for the creation?

Faced with the puzzle of natural evil and the ancient lineage of the problem of theodicy, and bearing in mind the centuries of false prophets who have claimed to know God's will all too well, I think we must be very, very modest in answering this question. Given the centrality of the divine-human drama in Christian faith, given its proclamation of the redemptive event addressed to humankind, I am certainly willing to say —more than willing, in fact, insistent upon saying—that our focus must be on human life, and that our task with the earth is to sustain the conditions for human life for as far into the future as our wits and strength allow. But I am not willing to go much beyond that. I am not willing to guess at what the earth's good is, or, to put it better, to guess at what God intends for the earth, which by definition would be its good.

A Calculus of Rights

The biocentrists are much less modest. They do claim to know the good of nature. If I may turn the tables on them, I would say they are far more daring, even impudent, in their claims to know the purposes of nature (or of God with nature, if they are theists) than are traditional Christians. Building on their theory of intrinsic value in natural entities, the biocentrists tell us that there are severe limits on what we may do with the natural world. In search of a strong position that will have sufficient force to restrain human selfishness, many of them, though not all, adopt the language of rights. Nature has rights, and thus has claims against us, much as we human beings claim rights that other human beings may not transgress.

But at once they plunge us into a realm of competing rights. Whose rights take precedence? When may they be violated, and by whom? May we eat meat? experiment on animals in laboratories? spread agricultural pesticides? use antibiotics? dam rivers? May a cat kill a mouse? In order to solve these conflicts and save the whole concept from reduction to absurdity, its defenders propose an inequality of rights, or even a complete disjunction between our obligations to one another and to the natural world.

Constructing a calculus of variable rights for different levels of existence is no simple task, however. Nash, who calls himself a Christian biocentrist and who, for his theological care, deserves to be exempted from many of the faults of the larger movement, does it by using "value-creating" and "value-experiencing" as the criteria for relevant differences, with rights diminishing as we descend a scale established by the relative presence of these capacities. Thus he hopes to solve conflicts of rights by "appropriate adjustments for the different contexts."[20] Rolston similarly would have the rights of animals and other natural entities "fade over a descending phylogenic spectrum."[21] These systems give priority in rights to human beings, a lesser preference to creatures merely sentient, and still less to non-sentient entities.

More radical versions of rights in nature take a Schweitzer-like approach, avoiding all killing of "lesser" forms of life except under threat to our own lives, and then only with a profound sense of sorrow for this necessary evil. How many times have we heard it said in recent years, with wondering admiration, that American Indians, those supposed ecological paragons, apologized to their game before killing it? An Irish pacifist once told me, with appropriate sardonic tone, that political assassination in Ireland was so common it was considered a normal part of the political process rather than murder in the sense of violating the sixth commandment; "but," he added, "it is doubtful whether the victims appreciated the distinction." And so also the caribou, slain by an Indian arrow tipped with a profound apology.

Faced with these tangles, even the biocentrically inclined must be tempted to give up on rights language. Rolston verges on the cynical when he admits that rights may after all be merely "a cultural discovery, really a convention" that does not translate to ecosystems, but that it may be politically useful to use the term anyway. "It is sometimes convenient rhetorically but in principle unnecessary to use the concept of rights at all." [22] What matters is the power of the restraint, and the language may be adjusted as necessary.

Reining in Rights

With all due respect to the intellectual strength and agility of the biocentric arguments, I would slice through their Gordian tangles by limiting "rights" to intrahuman affairs. "Rights" is a political and social term in the first instance, applicable only to human society, often enshrined in a fundamental document like a constitution, or embedded in the common law. As a metaphysical term, the transcultural phrase "human rights" applies to that which belongs to human beings by their very nature, i.e., not by their citizenship. Theologically, we guarantee human rights neither by our nature nor by our citizenship but by the radical equality of the love of God, the concept of "alien dignity," a grace bestowed on us that does not belong to our nature as such. In none of these forms has nature participated in rights.

Biocentrists sometimes seek to redress what to them are these deficiencies in the history of ideas by what I will call the argument from extension. "Rights," they point out, originally applied only to male citizens; but just as rights were gradually extended to women, to slaves, and finally to all other human beings, so it is a logical extension of this political liberalism to extend rights now to non-human creatures and even to agglomerations like ecosystems. Or, if the forum is not politics but Christian ethics, one could argue that the command to love our neighbors must now apply to non-human "neighbors," our "co-siblings of creation,"[23] or that the justice we are obliged to dispense to the poor and oppressed must now be extended to oppressed nature, or even that the enemies we are asked to love may include nature in its most hostile modes.

Although I appreciate the generous spirit of this line of argument, I think it involves a serious category mistake. Non-humans cannot have the moral status that only human beings possess, by our very natures. It is not irrelevant that the command to love our neighbors, in its original context, does in fact *not* apply to non-humans. An "extension" amounts to a substantial misreading of the text. Our obligations to the natural world cannot be expressed this way.

Another use of the idea of extension, one that occurs in Nash and in a different way in Paul Santmire,[24] is to argue that ultimate redemption is meant not only for humankind but also for the natural world, indeed the whole cosmos. That would imply much about our treatment of nature, our companion in cosmic redemption. The Incarnation confers dignity not only on us but on the whole material world: the divine takes on not only human flesh but material being in general. Certain New Testament passages are suggestive here—Romans 8:18-25, Colossians 1:15-20, Revelation 21:1—and Eastern Orthodox theology has formally incorporated this notion.

This is a theological idea of considerable gravity, and it deserves to be taken seriously. Nevertheless the doctrine is only vaguely expressed and appears to faith as hope, a hope made legitimate by faith, but a hope without details. Indeed, if we are to be scientifically honest, it is a "hope against hope," given the secular geological wisdom about the death of planet earth in fire and ice. The doctrine of eschatological renewal cannot tell us much about the care of nature beyond what we already know from our stewardship obligation, that we are to preserve this world as a habitat fit for humanity. The natural details of a redeemed environment are beyond our ken. Our trust in God for the eternal Presence beyond death does not require the preservation of these rocks and rills, these woods and templed hills. Again we find ourselves behind the veil of ignorance: we simply do not know nature's divine destiny.

In short, and in sum thus far, I believe it would be more consistent, more logical, and conceptually much simpler to insist that nature has neither intrinsic value nor rights. And I believe this is true whether we are secular philosophers or Christian theologians, whether we speak with the tongues of men or of angels.

Policy Consequences of Biocentrism

It is time now to ask what is practically at stake in this disagreement. What are the policy consequences of the biocentrists' position, for which they seek the vocabulary of rights or other strong language? What is denied to us thereby that would be permitted from the viewpoint of Christian humanism?

Since the biocentrists will not allow us to use nature as we see fit for ourselves, but insist that it has rights or at least claims of its own against us, their general recipe is that it should be left alone wherever possible. There is of course disagreement about the details and the exceptions, but the presumption is in favor of a hands-off policy. That is the *prima facie* rule: Let nature take its course. The burden of proof is on us to show why we should be allowed to impose our wills on natural processes.

Concretely this means we should take the necessary measures to protect existing species for their own sakes, not because they might offer something to us in the form of, say, aesthetic pleasure or possible future medicinal benefits. The Endangered Species Act should be vigorously defended and enforced; and its conflicts with human desires—the spotted owl vs. the timber industry, the snail darter vs. the Tennessee dam—should be settled in favor of the species threatened. The state will have to intervene to protect the species and the land, which means limitations on a landowner's use of his own property. After all, the wild animals and plants on the land should have their freedom, too.

Especially should we preserve and expand wild lands, the necessary larger habitats needed for these species, even though human beings may desire the land for other purposes, like farming. When it comes to such conflicts, mankind ought to lose. Arne Naess, founder of the Deep Ecology school (which is a form of biocentrism tending to argue the equal worth of all natural entities), says with astonishing frankness, "If [human] vital needs come in conflict with the vital needs of nonhumans, then humans should defer to the latter."[25]

We should also leave alone those injured wild creatures that we are tempted to save—the baby bird fallen from its nest, the wounded animal we come upon in the forest, the whale trapped by the ice. Intervention in natural processes is wrong whether the motives are benevolent or not. The species is strengthened by the premature extinction of its weaker members. Respecting nature's integrity means not imposing our soft-hearted human morality upon it. We should let forest fires burn and have their way with the wild creatures.

We should not build monuments in the wild. No more Mount Rushmores, no Christ of the Andes, no railroads up Mount Washington, and probably no more wilderness roads or ski lifts.

We should suspend genetic engineering in agriculture and animal husbandry and not permit there anything we would not permit among human beings. We should not take animal lives in teaching biology or medicine, and certainly not in testing cosmetics. Zoos and botanical gardens are suspect; better that the species there displayed should live in the wild. We should not keep pets. (There go my Springers.)

What about recreational hunting or fishing? Some biocentrists frown upon it as human interference with nature and unnecessary to our diet besides; but others would permit it as simply a form of predation, which is a fact of nature and not subject to our moral scrutiny. And by this same token there would be no moral obligation for us to become vegetarians. In fact, and rather awkwardly, even plants have a "good of their own" in the biocentric theory, which leads to some mental agility to sort out their permissible uses. It is all right to eat them, of course, for that is nature's way; but "frivolous" uses (Halloween pumpkins? Christmas trees?) are questionable. One suspects that even flower gardens would be a dubious activity, which may be why the biocentric literature rarely if ever mentions them.

Although we are in principle to leave nature alone, we are obligated to restore that which we have harmed. This form of intervention is acceptable because it is guided by the principle that pristine nature, before human impact, is somehow ideal. Here again the calculus of permissibility has to be rather finely tuned. It might be wrong to plant trees in a natural desert, for example, but obligatory to plant them if human activity had contributed substantially to creating that desert. Obviously this principle can be carried to extremes. Paul Shephard has seriously suggested that we in this country all move to the coasts and restore the land between to its pre-human condition, in which we would be permitted only as hunter-gatherers, like our most primitive ancestors. Few biocentrists would go anywhere near this far, but the principle is there. The argument is about the movable boundaries.

Stalking the Elusive Limits

My criticism of these limits begins with their vagueness and ambiguity, which is spiced with a generous dash of arbitrariness. Species, we are told, should be allowed to exist until the end of their natural "evolutionary time"; but how can we know when that time has arrived? We human beings should not take more than our "due" or occupy more than our "fair share" of land or exceed our "limits" in technological grasp; but these terms cannot even begin to be specified. What can be done with any creature turns on its degree of neural complexity, or some other hierarchical principle; but such distinctions will never be clear and are subject to a lot of pure arbitrariness. In the end I suspect that these measures are not in nature, but in ourselves. The lines are drawn according not to objective natural differences but to human preferences: human beings supply the values.

The matter of species disappearance is also confused. Leaving nature alone means allowing natural extinctions. Are we then to allow species to vanish, intervening only to save those threatened by human activity? (Yes, says Rolston. New life arises from the old when the demise is natural, but artificial extinction is "without issue."[26]) Or is it our responsibility to preserve as many species as possible, no matter what threatens them? Isn't domestication, far from being harmful interference with the wild, a useful way to preserve species? In defense of all of us dog owners, I note that many creatures have thrived because of the human presence—mice and rats, famously, and raccoons, and of course all species bred as pets or for agricultural utility.

The degree of simplicity of life is another matter of confusion. Some biocentrists would allow a fairly complex civilization. Others, like the bioregionalists, would turn their backs on the global economy and live in a locally sustainable way, even reverting to a simple agricultural economy. The movement as a whole can offer us very little real guidance about our permissible impact on the natural world. While it would allow us to feed and clothe and house ourselves, it would require of us some degree of self-limitation because of our exceptional talents, including particularly our talent for reproducing ourselves. But it is very difficult to tell what this directive might mean beyond the generalized complaint that we are too clever and thus exceed our space too readily. We have to pretend we are less, in effect, so that the other creatures may be more; but how and how much are quite unspecifiable.

The practical problems with the theory are many and are mainly intractable. They are also mostly unnecessary. Inevitably, once rights for non-human entities are proposed, the situation becomes impossibly complex. Absent this proposition, matters become much clearer, though solutions are seldom completely evident. We are still in for a process of experiment, of trial and error, mistake and correction. We have a lot to learn, mostly from science. But with a focus on human welfare we will have a reasonably clear idea how to use our knowledge; the complexities will be simpler, the conflicts easier to resolve.

Biocentric Fatalism: Many Must Die

There is one final, serious problem with biocentrism, and that is its fatalism. Biocentrists take their cues as to what *ought* to be from what *is,* and thus base their views of an acceptable future on what will happen if we let the natural world follow its own laws as far as possible. If an organism exists, the biocentrist presumes it has an important ecological niche and should be left alone. "Natural kinds are good kinds until proven otherwise."[27] If it is an ecological misfit it will perish naturally anyway, and we should not regret its demise. Death may be bad for individuals, but it is good for the system.

Should this ecological "wisdom," if that is the word, be applied to Homo sapiens? Because the whole direction of biocentric thought is to answer this question affirmatively, and because the consequences are so fearsome for most people's sensitivities, it is hard to find candid replies. When they do come out, ordinary ethical opinion, unenlightened by this new environmental realism, is apt to be appalled. Should we curtail medicine so that more of us may die "naturally" and earlier? Yes. Should we refrain from feeding the hungry, so that population will not exceed its boundaries? Yes, said the "lifeboat school," and especially its helmsman Garrett Hardin, whose bluntness is plainly an embarrassment to the current generation of biocentrists. Or consider J. Baird Callicott's rendering of William Aiken's questions as direct statements: "Massive human diebacks would be good. It is our duty to cause them. It is our species duty, relative to the whole, to eliminate 90 percent of our numbers."[28]

Even Lynn White, that most humane and Christian man, walked up to the edge of this moral abyss. Human beings are crowding out earth's other species, our "comrades" on the planet, and a balance needs to be restored. How shall we do this? Shall individual human beings be sacrificed, in defiance of traditional Christian ethics, if some killing will save many species? White hesitated, he said, to "light candles before the saints requesting a new Black Death" to give us, like fourteenth-century Europe before us, a "tragic respite" from our ecological peril. Almost visibly he drew back from the fearful answer; and yet with only slight obliqueness he said it: Many must die.[29]

To be sure, and to be fair, many biocentrists recoil from the social implications of their theory. It is only the biocentric egalitarians, for whom all life is of equal value, who are driven to these fearful antihuman conclusions. For the others, their schema of hierarchical differentiation allows them to claim a different level of moral behavior among human beings, different from that between human beings and the natural world, and certainly different from natural amorality. Callicott insists that "humanitarian obligations in general come before environmental duties." Rolston calls it "monstrous" not to feed starving human beings, though he would let overpopulated wild herds die.

But the boundaries between nature and culture are blurred and repeatedly crossed, as the examples of White and Hardin show well enough. Callicott acknowledges that the conflicts are a "difficult and delicate question." Nash calls them "immensely complicated." Rolston says that ecological "fitness" means and implies different things in nature than it does for human beings, but (let the reader beware) the two meanings have similarity, too; they are "homologous" or "analogous." "This biological world that *is* also *ought* to be; we must argue from the natural to the moral. . . . So much the worse for those humanistic ethics no longer functioning in, nor suited to, their changing environment."[30] Apparently one can, in a way, import ethics from nature to culture.

And that is precisely the ethical problem. Without a secure anchor in humanism, Christian or otherwise, biocentrism risks great moral evils. At the extreme, it appears actually indifferent to human destiny. Paul Taylor says that as members of a biotic community we must be impartial toward all species, our own included: that in fact we are unnecessary to other species that would be helped by our extinction. Thomas Berry is similarly minded: "The human species has, for some thousands of years, shown itself to be a pernicious presence in the world of the living on a unique and universal scale."[31] Since species must be allowed their "evolutionary time" and then die, and because this process is "good," the human species, too, must expect to perish; and from nature's point of view, that will be normal. If nature were capable of regret, there would be no regret for our passing. The ecosystem will survive as well or better without us at the top of the food chain. But since nature is amoral, we must say that our extinction is of no moral significance in nature.

Would God care? The whole direction of our faith says that God would indeed care, which suggests strongly that we should oppose biocentrism and not anticipate the demise of our species with equanimity. I admit that this is a conviction of faith. What God really is about I would not dare to say I knew.

Whether such modesty is becoming or not, it eludes the biocentrists, who seem to know more than I do about the ultimate principles that rule the universe. Here, for example, is Carol Christ:

> We are no more valuable to the life of the universe than a field [of flowers]. . . . The divinity that shapes our ends is an impersonal

process of life, death, and transformation. . . . The life force does not care more about human creativity and choice than it cares about the ability . . . of moss to form on the side of a tree. The human species, like other species, might in time become extinct, dying so that other lives might live.[32]

Rolston is only moderately more hopeful: the evolutionary system is "not just a random walk" but "some kind of steady, if statistical heading." In the extinction of some species and the appearance of new ones "a hidden principle seems to be at work, organizing the cosmos in a coherent way." But that is scant comfort to human beings, who come very late to the story and are only "short-sighted and arrogant" if they think it was meant for them.[33] Rolston is quite fatalistic about our destiny: recognizing that there is nothing necessary or inevitable about our appearance on earth, we will simply have to accept the overall course of evolution as good, no matter where it eventually goes.[34]

James Gustafson, a justly celebrated ethicist, has written similarly that we should not count on humanity's being at the apex of creation nor consider that human good trumps the good of non-human nature. Our disappearance would not be bad "from a theocentric perspective," which acknowledges that "the source and power and order of all of nature is not always beneficent in its outcomes for the diversity of life and for the well-being of humans as part of that." "The Divine . . . [is] the ultimate source of all human good, but does not guarantee it." Such ruminations have led Nash to characterize Gustafson's "God" as "a nonconscious and nonmoral ordering power without intention, volition, or cognition. . . . This power sustains the universe, apparently unintentionally, but lacks the purposive, benevolent, or redemptive qualities to seek the good of individuals, the human species, otherkind, or the whole cosmos. . . . This perspective seems close to atheism or pantheism."[35]

The ecological ethic emerging from biocentric fatalism, such as it is, is simply to enjoy the earth's fecundity, to laugh and weep and celebrate all life, whether it is our life or not. "Humanity's highest possibility is to bear witness to and participate in the great process of life itself."[36] And so the biocentrist love affair with a mysterious Natural Process cultivates, inevitably, indifference to the human prospect.

It is, of course, a bit odd for biocentrists to view humanity as just another species serving out its evolutionary time, when with the same voice they must also acknowledge that we are a very special species, endowed with enormous power over the environment. We cannot renounce this power, either. It is ours to use for good or ill, and so they urge us to use it in a self-limiting way to preserve the rest of the environment and to care for the other creatures of the earth. Notice that the message is anthropocentric in spite of itself: our great power engenders our great responsibility. But that, of course, is precisely the Christian ethic of dominion and stewardship.

I do not know where the human story will end. But, as I think William Faulkner, that great literary icon of my college generation, said in accepting the Nobel Prize, "I decline to accept the end of man." I think that my efforts ought to be bent to perpetuating human life, and that that goal ought to be the overriding test of our ecological conduct. In arguing otherwise, large sections of the environmental movement are on the wrong track. In the name of its own humanistic faith, Christianity ought to criticize these environmentalists, rather than scramble to say, "Me, too." What is historic and traditional in our valuation of Creation is a perfectly sufficient guide to sound ecology.

A Response

James A. Nash

Tom Derr is always a formidable thinker and dialogue partner, and always, when disagreements arise, a worthy opponent. His challenges must be taken seriously. Often they force the challenged to construct stronger arguments than they would have done otherwise. He is also unquestionably a committed environmentalist, as his record indicates. In this he is quite unlike those anti-environmentalists who may rally round his critique of some contemporary environmental philosophy and theology. Such people misinterpret his cause, which is the reform of environmentalism.

Nonetheless, counting myself an admiring and grateful friend who has been influenced by Derr's thought, I hope to lovingly demolish some of his major arguments.

My intention is not to defend biocentrism. I have at least as many criticisms as Derr does of thinkers whom he lumps together indiscriminately in this category. Though I have been perceived as a biocentric ethicist, and though I have given plenty of cause for that perception by highlighting biotic intrinsic values and a particular version of biotic rights (*biotic* referring to living organisms in general, while *anthropic* concerns only human life), I would not describe myself as strictly a biocentrist—particularly not as Derr defines (or misdefines?) that perspective. As I wrote in *Loving Nature:*

James A. Nash is executive director of the Churches' Center for Theology and Public Policy, in Washington, D.C. He is the author of *Loving Nature: Ecological Integrity and Christian Responsibility* (Abingdon, 1991).

> My own ethical perspective . . . cannot be described fairly as simply biocentric, ecocentric, or anthropocentric, to use the current code-words. None of these perspectives in isolation fits reality. All three have critical contributions to make to an adequate Christian ecological ethic. I, therefore, have tried to incorporate elements from all three into an integrated ethic.[1]

My purpose has been, not to replace anthropic values with biotic values, but rather to supplement the former with the latter and to weave them together coherently. My recent writings have focused on both human social and environmental rights and biotic rights.

Though Derr exempts me from many of the faults of biocentrism because of my alleged "theological care," I do not always feel exempted from his charges, because of his tendency to treat significantly different views as the same. In fact, a basic fault of his paper is an indiscriminate consolidation of contraries. That is, he lumps together a variety of disparate ethical perspectives on the basis of one criterion while neglecting many distinguishing criteria, and then criticizes the whole for the flawed perspectives of some of the parts—flaws that many who represent other parts of this artificial and unwarranted whole would reject as strongly as Derr does. A typology, with separate critiques of each type, could avoid his excessive and unfair generalizations.

However, I basically agree with a number of Derr's grievances about much environmental thought. I share his antagonism to what I've described as the "ecological complaint against Christianity," namely, that the Christian faith is the primary culprit in the ecological crisis.[2] That is truly "historical nonsense," as Derr argues—indeed, anthropological and logical nonsense as well, in light of the cultural and religious miscomparisons that are usually associated with this complaint. Christian traditions certainly have many ecological sins of omission and commission to confess, but there have been far too many interacting factors in ecological depredations to single out Christianity as the chief culprit. That interpretation also ignores the actual and potential contributions of Christian faith to ecological integrity. Fortunately, this complaint has been subsiding recently, partly as a consequence of the critical responses of Christian theologians and ethicists and the increased involvement of Christians in ecological causes.

I agree also with much of Derr's reaction to romantic views of nature—sentimental illusions about harmony and peace, for example. I think, however, that he sometimes overreacts and fails to see also the full ambiguities, including the positive and creative possibilities in human relationships with the rest of nature. Part, but only part, of the human condition is the struggle against the rest of nature for survival and the creation of cultures. Some "subduing" is necessary. The present problem, however, is subduing far beyond the point of necessity, imaging despotism rather than dominion, and abusing what is divinely designed for fair and frugal use. In this context, we can still talk about "loving nature," as I do, but it must be an interpretation of Christian love that is grounded in ecological realism, not the romanticism that Derr rightly rebukes.

Finally, I agree with many of his criticisms of particular interpreters of biocentric themes—including Lynn White, Jr., Garrett Hardin, Paul Shephard, Paul Taylor, Thomas Berry, Carol Christ, and Paul Ehrlich. But again I think he is wrong in lumping these interpreters together, let alone in grouping them with a number of contrary interpreters into a single category. Moreover, his criticisms of Holmes Rolston appear to oversimplify a complex and ambiguous body of thought. Rolston is a Christian theist as well as a distinguished philosopher who is reasoning with his peers on the basis of strictly philosophical methods.

Despite some areas of agreement with Derr, I also have some fundamental disagreements. These have to do with (1) stewardship, (2) theological foundations, (3) intrinsic value, (4) biotic rights, and (5) the social consequences of biocentrism.

1. Stewardship

Derr argues that the "real orthodox Christian attitude toward nature" is stewardship or trusteeship to God, the ultimate proprietor and provider. He sees the stewardship model now being replaced by the "powerful and pervasive school" of biocentrism, of which nearly all its diverse members view stewardship as "repulsively anthropocentric." Derr never defines the concept that is central to his ethic, but he suggests that stewardship means the use and management of the rest of nature solely for human sustainability. Nature's value is strictly instrumental for human needs. He sees biocentrism and stewardship as alternatives.

My quarrel with Derr and others is not about the centrality of stewardship for Christian ecological ethics, but rather about their exclusively anthropic and instrumentalist interpretation of stewardship. I have been very reluctant to use the concept of stewardship to describe human ecological responsibilities in some contexts precisely because of the contradictory interpretations on the current scene. The real debate about stewardship is whether it means loving care and service for the sake of both human beings and other life forms, or the technical management of the biosphere as a "resource base" solely for human needs. If stewardship means the former, as I think it does in many Christian interpretations, historical and modern, I happily accept it. If it means the latter, as it did for Gifford Pinchot and his followers who have been party to the secularization of the concept going on since the Enlightenment, I must reject it.

Stewardship in the former sense is quite compatible with the recognition of biotic values, though it is certainly incompatible with the misanthropy of biotic egalitarianism. The works by Douglas John Hall and by Loren Wilkinson and others—which Derr commends as models of the stewardship he defends—do not interpret stewardship and biotic values as alternatives. Both call for respect for the intrinsic value of non-human life.

2. Theological Foundations

Derr argues that the theological concept of cosmic redemption, which Orthodox theologians have always accepted and an increasing number of Protestant and Catholic theologians are now accepting, "cannot tell us much about the care of nature beyond what we already know from our stewardship obligation, that we are to preserve the world as a habitat fit for humanity." He suggests that the same is true of other Christian affirmations. On the contrary, the central affirmations of the Christian Church imply a great deal beyond the obvious obligation of stewardship that Derr supports. Respect for the intrinsic value of non-human life is coherent with basic Christian theological themes—indeed, to a far greater degree than any competing interpretations of ecological responsibilities. In my *Loving Nature* I have argued this point at length, in regard to several doctrines.[3]

In the doctrine of creation, for example, the Creator who is Love has made all creatures as acts of love and as recipients of ongoing love, endowing all with a moral status. In Genesis 1, the creation and its creatures are declared to be "good" *before* the emergence of Homo sapiens. In Psalm 104, God is praised for comprehensive benevolence to all creatures *apart from* any human values. God values the whole creation *apart from* any human utility in Job 38–41 (cf. Ps. 149:9). The logic of the doctrine of creation, with its stresses on divine sovereignty and universal providence, implies that the Creator is concerned about the well-being of the whole of creation and all its parts, not only with the human component. Ethically, since fidelity to God implies loyalty to divine valuations and affections, Christians are called to value what God values. We are called to be the images of God, responsible representatives who reflect the values of our Sovereign. Since, according to the New Testament interpretations of *imago dei,* Christ is the perfection of the image and the model of love, we are called to mirror the love of Christ toward all whom God loves. In this sense, stewardship—and dominion—is the representation of nurturing and serving love toward all God's beloved, not only humankind.

In the doctrine of the Incarnation, God entered into solidarity not only with humankind but also with the whole biophysical world that human beings embody and on which our existence depends. Christ is not only the Representative of God but the Representative of Humanity—and, therefore, the Representative of the Cosmos, the Cosmic Christ. The Incarnation confers worth not only on humanity but on everything with which humanity is united in interdependence. Exclusively anthropocentric valuations seem incompatible with the Incarnation. The doctrine justifies biophilia.

Through the sacramental presence of the Spirit, the world is filled with the glory of God. It is the medium of the Holy, the temple of the Spirit. Nature is sacred by association, as the bearer of the sacred. Nature is not divine and not to be worshipped; but it is still to be valued and loved in itself, since it is valued by God as the mode of spiritual presence and residence, God's beloved habitat.

Finally, the hope for cosmic redemption—rooted in Scripture (Isa. 11:6-9; 65:17, 25; Col. 1:14-20; I Cor. 15:28; Eph. 1:10; Rom. 8:19-22) and in the traditions of the first three or four centuries—gives ultimate meaning and worth to both human and non-human life. Every living creature counts not only for itself but for God. This hope is the ultimate confirmation of God's respect for the intrinsic value of all life. This perspective stands in judgment on anthropocentrism. If all life will participate in God's redemption, then all life forms must be treated with respect in accord with divine valuations, as ends in themselves, not simply means to human ends.

Thus, Christian understandings of God as Creator, Spirit, and Redeemer strongly suggest that divine valuations are not only anthropic but also biotic, each appropriate to its kind. Respect for biotic rights is theocentric respect for the biotic values of God.

Contrary to what Derr said, the fact that the command to love our neighbors is not applied to non-humans in the biblical texts does not prevent such extensions. The logic of love in Scripture and doctrine, as I have argued following Joseph Sittler and Albert Schweitzer, actually encourages such extensions to universal dimensions. There is no inherent reason why biblical norms cannot be extended to relationships between humanity and other living things. But there are very good reasons why this extension of love (including justice) is justified —notably the affirmation that God is universal love. The really serious ethical problem, however, is how to express this love in a predatorial biosphere, in which we must kill non-human creatures and destroy their habitats in order to survive and exercise our cultural creativity —how, in other words, to be *altruistic predators*.

3. Intrinsic Value

Derr is absolutely right in focusing his attack on the concept of the intrinsic value of non-human life, for that concept is the foundation of biotic rights. Unless entities have some values for themselves, rather than merely some instrumental values for others, they have no basis for moral claims for treatment appropriate to their value. They can have no moral rights, entailing human (and only human) moral responsibilities. But Derr is wrong, I believe, in his interpretation of intrinsic value and in his argument that the concept of biotic rights does not depend on certain attributes.

Although he directs his critique of intrinsic value and biotic rights largely at my interpretation, he ignores what I have argued is the one fundamental attribute necessary for recognizing intrinsic value and biotic rights: *conation.* I agree with Derr and others that rights cannot be assigned arbitrarily. They must have some reasonable basis. However, the basis of biotic rights need not be the same—indeed, cannot be the same—as the grounding of human rights in universal human equality. There is no reason why certain rights against the human community cannot be recognized on grounds other than human characteristics. There can be more than one basis for moral rights.[4] One need only establish a moral status that is sufficient to warrant appropriate moral treatment from the human community.

I find that basis or status in conation—that is, a striving to be and to do, characterized by aims *or* drives, goals *or* urges, purposes *or* impulses, whether conscious or non-conscious, sentient or non-sentient. At this point, organisms can be described as having "vital interests" (not in the sense of desires or preferences, but in the sense of needs or goods) for their own sakes. The planet's life forms, from unicellular to complex organisms, plants and animals, cannot be reduced to mechanized matter; they are at least systemic, interactive, adaptive, renewing, reproductive, evolving, and vital forces that struggle to fulfill their reasons for being. Indeed, they are miracles of life in an omni-miraculous world. Whatever other benefits or harms they produce for others, they are good for themselves, ends in themselves; they have intrinsic value.

Derr is certainly right in saying, as value theories assume: there cannot be a value without a valuer. But he misses the point of the intrinsic value of non-human life: *the valuer is the non-human organism itself for itself!* Its conation is the basis of its intrinsic value. Whether or not human beings should respect this intrinsic value of other life forms is another question, an extrinsic value judgment. On Christian theological grounds, however, as I have described them, and on other philosophical grounds, I believe we have firm obligations to honor the intrinsic values of all life forms. God loves/values the conative values that God has created, and that is a solid grounding for Christians to value them likewise. Of course, these assertions may be "immodest" or "impudent," as Derr mysteriously accuses Christian biocentrists of being in inferring God's purposes with the rest of nature from Christian affirmations. But if so, surely this inference is no more "immodest" or "impudent" than "insisting," as Derr does, that God's purposes are strictly anthropocentric. Seemingly, moreover, this inference is more coherent with central Christian affirmations, as well as with the ecological and evolutionary reality that human beings are parts and products of nature.

4. *Biotic Rights*

Derr clearly rejects the concept of biotic rights—and for good reasons. As the concept of moral rights for non-human life forms is currently interpreted in most of the popular and philosophical debates, I too reject it. The prevailing interpretations of non-human rights, by both advocates and adversaries, are ethically and ecologically distorted and indefensible. In fact, most thinkers in eco-philosophy strongly reject the concept of biotic rights. That includes Holmes Rolston, at least below the sentient level, contrary to Derr's interpretation. Moreover, most eco-philosophers would more accurately be described as "ecocentric holists," concerned about ecosystemic connections, rather than as "biocentric individualists," such as animal-rights advocates. That is an important distinction that Derr fails to note in combining the two, but it is a distinction that the two sides claim is fundamental in their continuing conflicts.

It is not my task to defend biotic rights here. I have, in any case, done that at length elsewhere.[5] But it *is* my task to respond to Derr's particular criticisms of the concept.

Biotic rights are certainly not the same full set of rights as human rights, nor are they equal with human rights. The two differ greatly in content and in the strength of the reasons to override them. Making human and non-human rights equal is inherently unjust, because this ignores the morally relevant differences in value-creating and value-experiencing capacities between humankind and all other species. Non-human life forms have only the moral claims against humans that are appropriate to the vital interests of their kind. Biotic rights deny the *exclusivity* of human values and rights, but they also affirm the *superiority* of human values and rights. They limit the exercise of some human rights, particularly economic rights, but they do not diminish or trivialize the fundamental importance of human social and environmental rights. Biotic rights are only *prima facie* claims, not moral absolutes. They can be overridden with a "just cause," which certainly includes vital human interests, though always within defined moral limits. Human and biotic rights are not alternatives; they can and do coexist coherently, contrary to Derr's suggestion.

The moral issues surrounding this extension of justice to the rest of the earth's living things are indeed mind-numbing in their novelty and complexity. It is sufficient here to note that if biotic justice is warranted, all life forms, individuals and species, have *prima facie* claims to a "fair share" of the goods, including the habitats necessary for their well-being. Of course, defining a fair share is extremely difficult, especially when, for our own well-being, human beings must destroy other life forms and their habitats. Yet it is a concept that we must struggle to define in order to stifle excessive human exploitation of the rest of nature.

In this process, we will encounter a variety of moral dilemmas inherent in the dual moral status of other species: as instrumental values for human needs, and as intrinsic values for themselves. Still, one conclusion seems clear: biotic justice imposes obligations on the human community to limit production and consumption in order to prevent the excessive commodification, domestication, and toxication of wildlife and wildlands. Profligate production and consumption are anthropocentric abuses of what God has designed for fair and frugal use in a universal covenant of justice.

The concept of biotic rights is complicated and still in an early stage of development. "Vague" and "ambiguous" criteria are certainly present, and I have been responsible for some of these; but vague and ambiguous criteria can in time be more sharply formulated. Unspecified norms are not necessarily unspecifiable, contrary to Derr. In fact, in the longstanding traditions of social ethics, ethical norms are rarely as specified as Derr seems to demand for ecological ethics. He is surely right to note some of the dilemmas and complications in biotic-rights theory and practice, but I think he is wrong to claim that the idea is "impossibly complex" and that the problems are "mainly intractable."

Equally, I think he is wrong to opt for a theory "conceptually much simpler." Ethical theories in general are becoming more complex, and human-rights theories are undergoing radical transformations from the Enlightenment inheritance. The appeal for simplification ducks the problem. If the moral claims of non-human life forms against the human community are valid, they cannot be ignored to minimize complexity. The truth cannot be simplified for the sake of intellectual convenience.

Similarly, Derr asserts, but does not argue, that the extension of moral rights to non-human life is a "serious category mistake." That is probably true of various popular and sentimental interpretations of these moral rights, but I think Derr would have a very hard time making that case against ethically serious interpretations, including my own. This charge, I think, would be true only if biotic rights were interpreted as being the same as or equal to human rights, but that is certainly not the argument of an ethically defensible case for biotic rights.

Derr wants to limit moral rights to intrahuman affairs. He makes no argument for doing so, only a series of undefended assertions. The appeal is primarily to tradition or the customary use of rights language. But the appeal to tradition gets us nowhere unless one can defend the validity of the tradition. In fact, the argument for biotic rights makes a rational break with the tradition, claiming that traditional usage is truncated. It argues that biotic rights can coexist comfortably with a strong set of human rights, as, in fact, I have tried to show elsewhere with a case for human environmental rights.[6]

In my continuing conversations with Derr on this question, I intend to probe him on his relationship with his Springer spaniels. Does he have obligations to them? On what grounds? Is his benevolence to them rooted in their moral claims on him? I remember a conversation with a student who thought biotic rights was an odd idea. I asked if she would strangle a baby robin in the nest, assuming she was not exceptionally hungry. "Of course not," she replied emphatically. "Why not?" I continued. "Because it has a right to be let alone," she answered, adding as an enlightened afterthought: "Oops!"

5. *Social Consequences of Biocentrism*

Derr describes some of the social consequences of non-human value and rights with *some* accuracy—for example, the protection of species for their sake as well as ours, the burden of proof on human interventions in ecosystems, and economic frugality. But he often leaves out important qualifications. And he tends to oversimplify and caricature at this point—for example, by claiming that biotic values imply the abandonment of zoos, animal experiments, pets, Halloween pumpkins, Christmas trees, and even the benevolent rescue of injured wild creatures. No doubt, some of these ideas have surfaced among a few proponents; generally they have not done so among serious thinkers unaccompanied by substantive arguments. But Derr gives no hint of these arguments. (And, frankly, I *hope* there are no more Mount Rushmores; the case against the one can be argued on strictly aesthetic grounds!)

Subsequently, however, Derr moves beyond oversimplifications and caricatures to serious accusations. He claims that biocentrism is inherently fatalistic and inevitably indifferent to human destiny. Human extinction is of no moral significance. On the question whether nature should be allowed to take its course in human affairs and, thus, whether human beings should curtail the use of medicines and refrain from feeding the hungry in order to follow "ecological wisdom," Derr claims that "the whole direction of biocentric thought is to answer this question affirmatively." These are the "social implications of [the] theory."

These are potent charges—and I believe indefensible charges against the vast majority of those who would describe their thought as biocentric or as having biocentric elements. For example, I drew very different conclusions in *Loving Nature.* No doubt, a very small percentage of extreme or pure biocentrists—or, far more likely, extreme ecocentrists, such as some "Deep Ecologists"—can be justly so accused, but surely not the vast majority of those whose thought can be described as biocentric or ecocentric. Again, Derr is critiquing collectively rather than typologically or individually. No wonder most biocentrists "recoil" from the alleged "social implications of their theory." The reason is that there are no such implications!

The alleged "social implications" simply do not follow, not inductively and certainly not deductively. Probably they do for the few "pure" biocentrists and ecocentrists. But the bulk of us are not pure in this sense (or in any other). In different ways and with different results, we have tried to integrate anthropic, biotic, and ecosystemic values into our social and ecological ethics, without jeopardizing our commitment to the human project. In fact, we believe that a commitment to biotic and ecosystemic values enhances the human prospect by preventing the excessive and imprudent destruction of the *human* habitat. Those of us who are Christians believe with Tom Derr that God cares deeply about the human prospects on this planet; but it does not follow logically that God cares *exclusively* about human prospects, or that biotic values cannot be integrated coherently with human values.

Overall, Derr's paper offers an important warning to those of us who have used the word "biocentric," perhaps loosely, to describe our ethical perspective. If the word connotes to some, as it apparently does to Derr, that the life process as a whole is "the primary locus of value," without moral distinctions among life forms and between human beings and all other life forms, then we need a better word to communicate our intentions more effectively. That connotation is clearly not what most of us intend, as our writings testify. Our intention is not to substitute biotic values for anthropic ones, but rather to supplement the latter with the former—to the enhancement of both. This integration of anthropic and biotic values, of social justice and ecological justice, is often called "eco-justice" in Christian circles.[7] I share that perspective.

Comments

Richard Baer: There's a certain irreverence to Tom Derr's paper that really troubles me. Maybe it's partly his characterizing Christians as anthropocentric. It seems to me that if we claim the label of Christian at all, we're theocentric. All these other categories are clearly subsidiary to being theocentric. This is more than a quibble. It somehow ties in with Derr's claim that the value doesn't belong to the object as such, that humans supply the value. In one ultimate sense, that applies to human beings also, that we have no value as such. We don't even remain in existence unless God holds us in existence. It's God who values us, and our value is derivative.

Having said that, I find it troubling to view God's creation as having just instrumental value, not intrinsic value. I'm interested in the Talmudic injunction, Do not destroy. There is wisdom in this. You do not destroy what you do not understand. If we were guests in somebody's house and didn't really know what the owner valued and what he didn't, it would be wise not to destroy things or claim they had no intrinsic value. I would want to err on the side of modesty.

But even more than that, I'm troubled by the claim that the value is entirely in the valuer. I think of C. S. Lewis's little book *The Abolition of Man*. We may disagree whether Bach is a better musician than Beethoven, but if anyone were to claim that Baer is a better musician than either Bach or Beethoven, that person would be demonstrating his ignorance about music. I think that we *can* make meaningful judgments about intrinsic value. Ultimately everything is valuable because God values it and has created it. You can make meaningful judgments about intrinsic value in natural objects, in oak trees and

Note: These participants are identified on pages 151-52.

elephants and such, that are not totally different from judgments we make about human beings. The position that humans supply the value, that value doesn't belong to the object, leaves us wide open to a total relativism or nihilism or skepticism, not just in morality but also in science and every other artifact of culture.

The position that nature has simply instrumental value leads us in a direction that is precisely what the biocentrists are worried about. I don't agree with the biocentrists, but they have something to teach us. I think they are reacting to a certain arrogance, a certain elevation of ourselves out of all proportion to who we are. There are very good reasons for not going in that direction and, if we don't want to use the term "intrinsic value," for at least arguing that God appears to value everything that he has created. We, of course, don't understand the role of everything from where we stand, and there is also a darker side to nature.

Thomas Derr: I wouldn't go around destroying things just because I don't believe they have intrinsic value. The doctrine of creation, which I believe in, saves me from that attitude. I am respectful of creation, but I don't believe it has intrinsic value. Its value is derivative from its Maker.

Craig Rucker: The Bible says some very pointed things about man's relationship to nature. In Genesis 1:28, God gives man dominion over everything on the earth; the text uses words like "subdue." In Genesis God ordains us to eat animals; clearly man is put on a higher plane than animals. The teaching of Jesus that man is worth more than sparrows—clearly here too there is an elevation of man above nature.

Richard Land: We have been talking about ecocentric, biocentric, anthropocentric understandings. It seems to me that as a Christian what I aspire to is a *theocentric* understanding that human beings have intrinsic value, not because we value ourselves, but because God valued us, and God has said: Don't be like the dumb animals; I will teach you, and you will listen and you will learn (Psalm 32). The theocentric view would say that the creation does not belong to us; it belongs to God. He has given us certain privileges and greater responsibilities: to protect it and also to till it, to guard it and also to develop it. Genesis 9 tells us that God made a covenant with every living thing: with human beings, with animals, with plants. Now at the same time he also told us we can eat animals and plants. But the covenant does say to us that God's creation has a God-given value that we cannot disregard. If I walk into a room and my son is dismantling the television set, I'm upset. If he's dismantling the dog, I'm much more upset. If he's dismantling his little sister, I'm horrified. These are meaningful distinctions. We do not have the right to treat a dog as if it were an inanimate object like a television set.

With biocentrism and ecocentrism, it is very easy to fall off into that terrible moral wasteland that we see in Eastern cultures, where they really have lost the ability to make meaningful distinctions between human life and animal life and plant life. They don't kill the rats that are eating the wheat that could feed starving people. The Bible makes a very meaningful distinction: all life deserves respect, but human life demands reverence. There is this firebreak between the two. I think we have a right to experiment on animals for reasons of human health but not for reasons of human beauty: to test human medicine but not to test human cosmetics. The latter is a frivolous disregard of the intrinsic worth of the life of an animal. We have the right to domesticate cows and to use them to feed human beings. We do not have the right to mistreat a cow, and we have an ethical responsibility to execute that animal as humanely as possible, with no needless suffering. God made a covenant with cows, just as he made a covenant with human beings.

Fred Smith: Let me introduce the concept of "ecological adoption." In the human situation, a child with no protectors is abandoned in a world of risk. As a last resort, the child becomes a property (the "ward") of the state. No one believes that this is a morally superior situation, so we create adoption mechanisms that allow private parties to come forward and say: We think we'd be better stewards of that child. The child is then moved from a state status to a private status. We privatize the child, in a sense.

Why don't we allow that option for endangered animals? E. O. Wilson argues that there could be as many as 100 million species on this earth that are at risk. There are 190 governments on the earth, most of which are doing an abysmal job of protecting their human populations. Do we really think these 190 political institutions are going to protect 100 million species? But there are 5.6 billion people on this earth, which means there are thousands of potential Noahs for every species out there.

Almost nothing survived until man came along. Almost 95 per cent of the species that have ever existed are gone today. Perhaps by legitimizing ecological adoption man can create a world in which 95 per cent of what is now around can survive.

5

Can Markets or Government Do More for the Environment?

Peter J. Hill

Environmental problems are traditionally seen as a result of market failure and as ample justification for government intervention. The pollution of air and water, the over-exploitation of land and other natural resources, and the extinction or near-extinction of species have led many analysts to conclude that government needs to involve itself in the economy much more directly and forcefully to solve these problems.

But it is an error to assume that, just because the market does not solve certain problems, government can effectively intercede to do so. To understand how markets and government interact, let us look first at the two institutions separately to see how they work and under what circumstances they fail.

Markets are best seen as systems of social coordination that allow mutual accommodation among people, most of whom have little personal knowledge of one another. Exchange in the marketplace facilitates social interaction and develops indexes of value that provide

---

Peter J. Hill is George F. Bennett Professor of Economics at Wheaton College, Wheaton, Illinois, and senior associate with PERC, Bozeman, Montana. He is the co-author, with Joseph L. Bast and Richard C. Rue, of *Eco-Sanity: A Common-Sense Guide to Environmentalism* (Madison Books, 1994).

guidance for individual and group decisions. To work well, markets need a set of clear and stable rules that form the basis for this social interaction. These rules, commonly termed property rights, specify who has authority to act with regard to a particular domain or resource.

Several aspects of property rights must be in place in order for those rights to provide the appropriate guidance to decision-makers. First, a well-functioning set of property rights connects actions to consequences; in other words, it provides accountability, or *liability.* Such a connection must hold people liable when they do things that impose costs upon other people. For instance, an effective property right regarding land would require the landowner's consent before any use is made of it. If I want to park my car on my neighbor's lawn, I need to secure his consent. As long as I have that consent—that is, if he has agreed to allow me to park there in return for monetary compensation, or simply because he likes me or wants to maintain good neighborly relations—then the marring of his lawn caused by the parking of my car will not be considered excessive.

A well-functioning property-rights system also requires *appropriability:* people must be able to appropriate the benefits of using their property in a way that advantages others. Again, this provides a connection between actions and consequences. Under current labor law in the United States, a person who works extra hours to accommodate the wishes of her employer is entitled to compensation. She can appropriate a stream of benefits from her actions and can exclude other people from benefiting from those actions without her permission.

A third aspect of a well-functioning property-rights system is *transferability.* Rights need to be fully transferable from one person to another if resources are to move to their highest valued use. Back to my neighbor's lawn and my desire to park my car there: if he places a value of five dollars a day on an unmarred, unparked-on lawn, but I value the opportunity of parking there at ten dollars, then a mutually agreeable exchange can be worked out—*if* the legal right of transferability is in place. If the rules do not allow him to transfer that right to me, then this opportunity for him to make money from this resource, his lawn, will be foregone.

When these aspects of property rights—liability, appropriability, and transferability—are in place, a flow of information develops that provides an accurate assessment of costs and benefits and enables people to take actions that are mutually profitable. The system also develops a set of incentives that encourage people to look for ways of accommodating others. We are able to live lives of freedom, harmony, and reasonable material comfort because of common understandings about the actions we can take and because we enter into cooperative arrangements every day. Without a way of generating information and encouraging mutual accommodation, human life truly would be "nasty, brutish, and short."

Because this mutual accommodation occurs through a spontaneous process of continual adjustment between people, we often fail to recognize how well it works. This adjustment process and the information it generates result from voluntary interactions among individuals, not from a deliberate, overall plan. Therefore it is easy to overlook how useful this interaction is, and to ignore the institutional and moral framework that makes it possible.

Where Markets Fail

Like all other institutions, however, markets have their shortcomings. During the last quarter of a century, the rising environmental consciousness in the United States has brought to light many examples of market shortcomings. In some areas of environmental concern the process of mutual accommodation is not working well, and the results of social interaction leave much to be desired. These shortcomings occur because decision-makers either lack adequate information or lack appropriate incentives. This is basically a property-rights failure; one or more of the aspects of property rights that we looked at earlier are not fully in place.

For instance, it is true that in order to park my car on my neighbor's lawn I have to secure his permission, and we get the socially correct amount of lawn parking because of the rule that I can park on his property only if he approves of it. But I have the option of using something else he values, his airspace, without securing his permission. I can drive back and forth in front of his house as often as I want to, pouring effluent from my tailpipe into his airspace, and he has no control over my actions. In this case, there is not a close connection between my actions and the consequences; I am not fully liable for what I do. In the jargon of economics this is an *externality,* or a situation where either some of the costs or some of the benefits generated by an action do not flow to the person who takes that action. In such cases, we do not get the socially desirable amount of activity. Because I can cause my neighbor to bear some of the costs of my driving my car, I will drive more miles than what is socially desirable.

Transaction costs are the reason for the divergence between private actions and social consequences. Why aren't the rights to air defined in the same way that the rights to land are? If we think of transaction costs as *the costs of defining and enforcing rights and carrying out exchanges,* it is obvious that these costs are much higher with some resources, such as air, than with others, such as land. We fail to have fully defined rights over certain resources because of high transaction costs, and in those cases the unfettered interaction of individuals will not produce the socially desirable amount of activity. Air and water pollution occurs because of the high transaction costs of defining and enforcing rights to these fugitive resources.

In the situation we have been considering, social interaction produces *too much* of something—namely, the driving of cars. However, in other cases high transaction costs make it difficult to carry out *enough* of certain activities. Assume that many American citizens have positive feelings toward the bald eagle. It may well be that every person in the country values bald eagles at ten dollars and would be willing to pay that amount rather than allow them to become extinct. People may feel this way even if they never expect actually to *see* bald eagles themselves. In this case, will the market provide for the eagles? It will be difficult for all citizens to come together to express their desire through market transactions. Some people may hide their desire for eagles and hope that others will provide for their preservation. These people can "free-ride" upon the actions of others, and because of that, voluntary transactions may not generate enough of the desired activity, eagle preservation.

Again, the problem is high transaction costs. The cost of excluding people who do not contribute to eagle preservation from sharing in the *benefits* of eagle preservation is high enough that it isn't carried out. The people who engage in preserving eagles cannot reserve the benefits of that activity exclusively for themselves. Thus the marketplace does not do an adequate job of compiling the preferences of all individuals; the high transaction costs of measuring those preferences causes the underprovision of certain goods.

All this analysis is standard fare in any economics text that deals with environmental problems. There is a well-developed paradigm for analyzing the failure of markets to provide for a quality environment. This failure is rooted in an institutional framework that generates inadequate information and inappropriate incentives for decision-makers. On the basis of such analyses, it is often said that government action is necessary to overcome these market imperfections.

Where Governments Fail

Certain developments over the last several decades, however, raise doubts about the ability of government to secure environmental quality. This is particularly the case when the government specifies certain outcomes while ignoring basic economic realities.

Our faith in government's ability to solve environmental difficulties has been weakened in two ways. First, empirical evidence from this country and around the world shows that when government has direct control over resources, its record is anything but ideal. Second, we now have a far better understanding than we used to about how government actually works and why bureaucracies often fail to achieve the goals for which they were created.

We need only to look at the U.S. Forest Service to see how ineffective the bureaucratic control of a resource can be. Millions of acres that are managed by the Forest Service have been logged, and their amenity value substantially decreased, despite the fact that logging hasn't paid and has gone on only because of large subsidies by the government. In Alaska's Tongas National Forest, the government spends ninety-eight cents for every two cents of timber harvested.[1]

Likewise, the Bureau of Reclamation has subsidized water projects that have flooded large areas and have had substantial environmental costs, and yet have continued to lose money on the irrigation water they have delivered to farmers. In 1993, for instance, Congress authorized completion of the Central Utah Project. Studies indicate that the project will deliver water to farmers at the cost of $350 per acre foot,[2] but that this water will generate only about $30 per acre foot of additional farm value.[3]

If government ownership of environmental resources were truly the best way to preserve those resources, then the formerly Communist countries of the Soviet Union and Eastern Europe, with their high degree of centralization and overwhelming governmental power, should have maintained a high level of environmental integrity. But, as we all know, what resulted instead was a level of environmental degradation that makes our own problems pale into insignificance.[4]

In the face of environmental disasters in the centrally planned economies of the former Soviet Union and Eastern Europe and the less dramatic but nevertheless disheartening results of government control in the United States, it is useful to apply to government the same analytical tools that help us understand why markets are imperfect social institutions.

As we saw above, high transaction costs sometimes prevent decision-makers in the marketplace from having adequate information and incentives. But transaction costs can be high in government as well.

Government, the one agency in society that has a legitimate monopoly on coercion, can be useful in reducing the costs of interaction among individuals. Like markets, government can improve the coordination of human activity, and its coercive powers enable it to overcome some of the difficulties that plague purely voluntary relations. However, such coordination requires, again, the communication of information and the generation of adequate incentives for action. Structuring government so that it acts appropriately entails substantial costs. Let us consider four areas in which transaction costs prevent government from being an effective solution to environmental ills: incentive problems, information-generation problems, the problem of diffuse costs and concentrated benefits, and the bundle-purchase problem.

1. Incentive Problems

The incentive problem is well illustrated by the Forest Service example. A district supervisor of the U.S. Forest Service has strong incentives to allow logging, because that increases the size of the Forest Service's budget, and his own advancement, power, and salary are all closely related to that budget size. Building roads and letting timber contracts is very much in the self-interest of the Forest Service bureaucrat. Although numerous reforms have been suggested to give Forest Service decision-makers more appropriate incentives, so far none have been implemented.

Other federal agencies have similar incentive problems. The Bureau of Reclamation clearly has had strong incentives to build dams and construct irrigation projects even where these have not made economic or environmental sense. Officials faced a reward structure that encouraged them continually to seek out new projects, underestimating the costs and overestimating the benefits in order to get them approved. The transaction costs of appropriately structuring bureaucratic incentives are high; as a result, the bureaucratic agency may do things that make the problem worse rather than solving it.

The incentive problem plagues most of government, not just bureaucratic agencies. In the 1970s and 1980s there was considerable concern about acid rain. In response, Congress passed numerous laws and in 1980 authorized a ten-year, $500 million study of the problem. The research effort, called the National Acid Precipitation Assessment Program (NAPAP), involved hundreds of scientists conducting extensive laboratory and field investigations around the country. By 1987, a preliminary version of the report was available, but political considerations delayed its final release until after the 1990 Clean Air Act Amendments had been passed. Those amendments will probably cost consumers between $29 billion and $39 billion a year while yielding environmental benefits worth about half that much.[5]

Why did Congress act without waiting for the report it had funded and asked for? By 1990 there was considerable political pressure to take action, almost any action, and there was little incentive for Congress to base its action upon sound scientific information. The political process rewards perception more than substance, and the fact that the NAPAP report would have made it more difficult to pass the Clean Air Act Amendments gave Congress a strong incentive not to want the information to be readily available. The NAPAP final report, entitled *Acidic Deposition: State of Science and Technology,* cast significant doubt upon the presumed extent of environmental damage from acid rain and the presumed degree to which acid lakes resulted from air pollution. Nevertheless, the incentives to act were strong, and Congress did so.

2. *Information-Generation Problems*

Closely related to the problems of structuring government so that decision-makers face appropriate incentives are the difficulties of generating good information. Often the two are closely related, as in the NAPAP acid-rain study. In that case, reasonably high-quality information was available, but the pressures of the political process prevented members of Congress from using that information. However, in other cases adequate information is not available for decision-makers, or they have little incentive to look for it.

Often the signals received from the political process are difficult to evaluate. Do ten letters to the editor of the local newspaper equal one testimony at a public hearing? Do five visits to a senator by environmental activists represent more demand than $5,000 in contributions from a forest-products political-action committee? There are no ready indexes of value, no reasonable mechanisms for making trade-offs among competing demands. Therefore, the political process often creates policies that ignore relevant trade-offs and do not pass the simple benefit-cost test.

An example of the failure to examine alternatives and seriously consider trade-offs is the Corporate Average Fuel Economy standards, which require rising fuel efficiency for American automobiles. These standards, originally devised because of the fear of running out of oil, now make much less economic sense, since there is no worldwide petroleum shortage. Also, important trade-offs were ignored in the policy discussion process. Research by Robert Crandall at the Brookings Institution and John Graham at Harvard University estimates that each year 2,200 to 3,900 deaths and 20,000 serious injuries that occur in traffic accidents are due to the smaller size and lighter weight of cars.[6] Making cars smaller and lighter was a rational response by car manufacturers to the fuel-efficiency regulations; but the question whether the loss of approximately 3,000 lives a year is worth the saving in fuel was never seriously debated in Congress or the regulatory agency. The political process has few reality checks on the flow of information. Those using the information have little incentive to check its reliability, or to assess the importance of one aspect of the information flow relative to the other aspects.

This is well illustrated by the approach to risk management by government agencies. Once an agency is charged with handling a particular set of risks, it has a strong incentive to minimize those risks with little attention to the real cost of its actions or to the potential higher return from using the same dollars to reduce risk in another arena. The table on page 129 estimates the cost per death averted by various risk-reduction policies. Although there is considerable evidence that we are spending billions of dollars to reduce certain risks when those same dollars would be far more effective in other areas, government agencies pay scant attention to such trade-offs.

Cost Per Death Averted By Risk-Reduction Policies

Activity	Cost per death averted
Third World Countries	
Diphtheria immunization (Gambia)	$87
Malaria prevention (Africa)	440
Measles immunization (Ivory Coast)	850
Improved health care	1,930
Improved water sanitation	4,030
Dietary supplements	5,300
United States, Non-environmental	
Improved traffic signs	$31,000
Cervical cancer screening	50,000
Improved lighting	80,000
Upgraded guard rails	101,000
Mobile intensive-care units	120,000
Breakaway sign supports	125,000
Lung cancer screening	140,000
Breast cancer screening	160,000
United States, Environmental	
Asbestos ban	$110,700,000
Benzene NESHAP (revised: waste operation)	168,200,000
1,2 dichloropropane drinking-water standard	653,200,000
Hazardous-waste land disposal ban (1st 3rd)	4,190,400,000
Municipal landfill standards (1988 proposed)	19,107,000,000
Formaldehyde occupational exposure limit #2	86,201,800,000
Atrazine/Alachlor drinking-water standard	92,069,700,000
Hazardous-waste listing for wood-preserving chemicals	5,700,000,000,000

Source: Joseph L. Bast, Peter J. Hill, and Richard C. Rue, *Eco-Sanity: A Common-Sense Guide to Environmentalism* (Lanham, MD: Madison Books, 1994), 162.

3. *Diffuse Costs and Concentrated Benefits*

A basic reason why government does not respond as we would like to information flows is that not all information is treated as equal by those affected by government programs. Most programs have costs that are spread over a large number of people but benefits that are concentrated upon a small group. Therefore it is hard to organize those who bear the costs of the program, while those who capture the benefits find it easy to make their position known. As a result, both the legislative branch and the executive branch of government find it difficult to balance the benefits and costs of a proposed program.

In the 1970s there was a great deal of concern over air pollution, particularly that caused by sulfur oxides from coal-fired power plants. Strong pressure was exerted on Congress to pass new regulations, and in 1979 the Environmental Protection Agency set its standards for coal burners. This would seem to be a straightforward problem that government could solve rather easily: it could raise the cost of sulfur emissions so that those burning coal faced the true social cost of their decisions.

However, the government process did not work so smoothly. Coal from the eastern and western parts of the United States differs in composition: eastern coal contains much more sulfur. Once it became clear that some sort of regulation of coal-burning plants was coming, the eastern coal interests mounted a strong lobbying effort and convinced EPA to mandate smokestack scrubbers on all coal-fired generating plants. Scrubbers are an effective but very expensive way of removing sulfur from smokestack emissions. In many cases, it would have made sense for utilities to switch from the high-sulfur coal of the east to low-sulfur coal from the west; emissions would have been reduced more and at less cost than with scrubbers. But once scrubbers were in place, the western low-sulfur coal no longer had a competitive advantage, and the economic interests of the eastern coal producers and labor unions were protected.[7]

Although the technology that was mandated made little economic sense, it was chosen because it spread the *costs* of the technology widely, over the population as a whole. Everyone paid more for utility generation and received less in the way of pollution reduction than could have been obtained by alternative methods. However, the *benefits* of the scrubber technology were heavily concentrated upon a particular group of people, the coal producers and workers from the eastern United States. Their effective lobbying resulted in a very costly way of achieving pollution reduction.

Time and time again, as government has attempted to deal with environmental problems, special interests have forced the mandating of more expensive and less effective pollution-reduction techniques.[8] The results of the political process rarely look anything like what was conceived of by those who thought government could easily solve a problem through some form of regulation, taxes, or subsidies.

4. The Bundle-Purchase Problem

In dealing with environmental problems we face uncertainty about which resources should be used and at what rate, and what technologies are appropriate. Both markets and government are mechanisms by which people assess the future and take action to shape it. However, the nature of the decision-making process yields very different results under these two mechanisms. Markets give individuals the opportunity to act upon their private preferences and to bet against prevailing wisdom. Market decision-making tends to produce diverse results, with a wide spectrum of viewpoints represented. Government decision-making, because of the difficulty of assessing different preferences and allowing for minority viewpoints, tends to produce less diverse results.

Which institutional mechanism should we choose to deal with environmental problems? It depends a great deal on how confident we are that we have the correct answers to those problems. If scientific opinion is in full agreement as to what resources to save and the best technologies to use, then government can effectively implement that knowledge. Majority rule prevents a few dissidents from sabotaging the process or using resources in ways that the majority knows to be incorrect.

However, if we are uncertain about the answers, if we are involved in an ongoing discovery process, it may be useful to choose a system that allows individuals to express their beliefs about appropriate use, even if they represent a distinct minority. The transaction costs of giving that minority a voice are much lower in a private-property system than when decisions are made by government.

Consider the differences in attitudes towards bird species that prevailed in the 1920s. During that period a leading conservationist, Rosalie Edge, became concerned that most conservation groups gave little attention to the preservation of birds other than songbirds and game birds. She was particularly disturbed about the slaughter of raptors—birds of prey, such as hawks and eagles—as they migrated down the Appalachian Mountains. Hawk Mountain in eastern Pennsylvania was an especially popular spot for hunters to go to kill eagles, ospreys, hawks, and falcons.

Edge represented a distinctly minority viewpoint. Had she attempted to use the political process, it probably would have been decades before she could convince a majority of the population to adopt her view. But she did not have to rely on the democratic process: she had to deal with only one person, the owner of Hawk Mountain. He sold her the land, she closed it to hunting, and the raptor population benefited substantially.

The story of Hawk Mountain is not unique. Many times in our history the majority of the population has opted for the rapid use of a resource, and only a few far-sighted persons have prevented complete destruction. The actions of the few were dependent upon a private property-rights system that allowed them access to the endangered resources even when they didn't have majority approval.

Of course, markets have also led to mistakes, when resources were exploited too rapidly or inappropriate technologies were used. However, that has usually been the result of inadequate property rights; that is, the resource in question was an open-access resource. In such cases policy changes that create more complete private rights can be helpful.

Toward a More Balanced View

In the past, most of the discussion of institutional responses to ecological problems has concentrated on the failure of markets and the hope of government solutions. A more realistic perspective recognizes that both markets and government have their shortcomings. Transaction-cost analysis help us to understand why this is so, why both government and markets may fail to give us the results we want. Transaction-cost analysis also helps us to design workable solutions.

Effective property rights are essential for achieving environmental quality; such property rights hold people accountable for the actions they take that disadvantage others, and allow people who take positive steps that increase social cooperation to capture the benefit of these steps. These property rights must be transferable so that the costs of using the environment are minimized and useful trades between people can occur. Since transaction costs prevent the complete definition and enforcement of these property rights, government action should focus upon being a transaction-cost reducer.

This perspective yields several important conclusions. First, government ownership of resources has little chance to succeed. The information and incentive problems of such ownership are well illustrated by the environmental debacle of the centrally planned economies of the former Soviet Union and Eastern Europe, and by the unsatisfactory record of government control of resources in the United States. Those charged with managing such resources rarely face adequate incentives to heed the true social costs of their actions, and the information they have to act upon is usually partial and incorrect.

Second, the command-and-control type of regulations, where government attempts to mandate technologies or to require all producers to reduce pollution by a fixed percentage or amount, are also likely to be a very costly way of dealing with environmental problems. Again, the transaction costs of appropriately structuring the incentives for the regulators are extremely high, and since command and control does not depend upon prices, information needed for sound decisions is lacking.

Finally, effective government solutions will be those that reduce the transaction costs of defining, enforcing, and exchanging property rights. In some cases, simply removing legal barriers to exchange can be very effective. Many California municipalities, faced with water shortages, have pressed for environmentally destructive and extremely expensive new water projects to meet their needs. However, water is available from nearby agricultural users at a cost much lower than that of the proposed water-delivery projects.[9] Removing the federal restrictions on water marketing would allow water to go to its highest valued use with considerable saving of resources and much less ecological damage.

In other cases, government can reduce transaction costs by using its coercive power to improve property rights. For instance, there is a continuing problem of over-fishing in the world's oceans because people do not have secure property rights. As a result, there has been a substantial decrease in the fishing stocks in certain areas. In the North Sea, incomes of British fishermen have fallen by 6 per cent (in real terms) since 1980, and the stocks of cod and haddock have decreased by one-half and two-thirds respectively.[10]

The property-rights framework suggests a possible solution to this problem. Individual transferable quotas, or ITQs, are a way of establishing more secure rights. ITQs assign each fisherman a right to a proportion of the catch and thus eliminate the incentive to over-fish the resource. The market establishes a price for the quota, and transferability allows the more efficient fishermen to buy out those who are less efficient. Both Australia and New Zealand have applied ITQ systems for particular species with considerable success. Six months after Australia instituted ITQs for its blue-fin tuna fishing, fleet capacity fell by 60 per cent, the value of quotas doubled, and larger fish were caught because operators with access to larger fish bought out operators with access to smaller fish.[11]

Pollution problems can also be substantially reduced through improvment of the property-rights framework. Common-law tort remedies can deal effectively with certain forms of polluting. When damage can be shown, the polluter must either stop the damage-causing activity or secure permission from those harmed. In England, people with fishing rights have used tort remedies to prevent upstream factories from harming the quality of their fishing by polluting the water. A group called the Anglers' Cooperative Association has a twenty-year record of dealing with pollution through common law. It has handled more than 1,500 cases and has recovered hundreds of pounds of damages for particular harms.[12]

Of course, it is important to note that such uses of the common law do not prevent all pollution. In the case of the English fisheries, if the upstream users were willing to pay enough, the downstream property-rights holders would allow a certain amount of pollution. Thus the use of resources is directed towards their highest value. If some pollution is appropriate, resource owners will trade rights until the additional cost of the pollution exceeds the additional benefits of the polluting activity. At that point, trades will cease.

There is also substantial potential for government to ameliorate water pollution through the common law. For instance, it is now possible to brand pesticides and fertilizers by adding chemical tracers or radioactive isotopes. All users could be required to register their particular brand at the time of purchase, and if water pollution occurred, those harmed could use the courts to secure compensation.

This same technique, one in which the government lowers the transaction costs of defining and enforcing rights, has potential application in air pollution. In the Winter Hayes Intensive Tracer Experiment in Canyonlands National Park, Utah, tracers were used to follow the course of air pollution.[13] Chemical tracers that mimicked the pollutant were introduced into the stack of a coal-fired generating plant several hundred miles from the park, and monitoring stations were able to determine the degree of pollution of air in the park caused by the generating plant. Effective monitoring of this sort could be introduced for all major industrial polluters.

There is an important distinction between government action of this sort—action that uses the framework of transaction costs and property rights to solve environmental problems—and the command-and-control methods so often proposed by advocates of government intervention. The simple definition and enforcement of rights allows individuals acting in their own self-interest to develop their own solutions. Prices are generated by the interaction of people who hold the property rights and those who wish to secure these rights, and the appropriate rate of resource use comes about without government control. Since much of the information that is necessary to solve pollution problems is time- and place-specific, the interaction of property-rights holders is likely to be far superior to any attempts by a government bureaucracy to determine appropriate rates of use and optimal amounts of pollution.

The transaction costs of structuring incentives and generating information plague attempts to deal with environmental problems through command-and-control regulations. Even if the agency is able to determine the appropriate level of pollution, there is no assurance that the level should remain fixed over time, and that the agency will be able to generate enough information to modify it appropriately. It is likewise difficult to structure bureaucratic incentives so that decision-makers can determine appropriate levels that really do reflect the desires of society. In contrast, if property rights can be established or quasi-rights can be enforced, the court system can be used to hold people responsible for the damages they impose upon others. The subsequent contracting among people will allow for continual adjustments in preferences and in pollution-control technology.

As we wrestle with the problem of environmental degradation, we need to be sensitive to the strengths and failures of various institutional arrangements. For too long we have portrayed markets as the problem and government as the solution. But the same problems that plague markets also plague government. Therefore, we need to use government very carefully and selectively if it is to deal effectively with market shortcomings in matters of the environment.

A Response

Andrew Steer

Peter J. Hill attempts to show why governments often do a poor job of managing the environment and why the market can do a good job. He is more effective at the former than the latter. The four reasons he gives for the inadequacies of the traditional "coercive" approach to environmental policy are certainly well taken. Had those who designed the U.S. environmental regulatory framework twenty-five years ago taken to heart such warnings, the United States could probably have saved half the cost of the cleanup—about $100 billion per year—and still have achieved the same degree of environmental improvement.

But while I agree with the fundamental warnings of the inadequacies of command-and-control policymaking and with the demonstrated benefits of the market, I disagree that we need to choose between the two. Rather, the "pragmatic approach," which harnesses market power and uses coercion where necessary, is often, in my view, exactly what is needed.

The starting point, of course, should be the power of market forces to influence behavior. There is *enormous* evidence that moving from distorted markets towards free markets can have huge benefits for the environment. Today this is hardly disputed by environmentalists. At the World Bank, we have demonstrated that eliminating energy subsidies in Eastern Europe and the former Soviet Union would eliminate half of all air pollution there, and would reduce global carbon emis-

---

Andrew Steer is director of the Environment Department of the World Bank.

sions by 9 per cent. All over the world, governments subsidize inputs and resource use at great cost to the environment. Logging is subsidized, leading to over-logging. Water is subsidized, leading to the depletion of aquifers and to waterlogging and salinization in irrigated agriculture. Pesticides are subsidized, leading to all kinds of damage to ecosystems and human health. These subsidies generally do not promote development, and they rarely benefit the poor. Moving towards free markets is good for environment, for development, and for the public purse—a win-win-win policy change!

What is true for subsidies is true for trade distortions also. Distorted, protective trade regimes, especially in developing countries, lead to older equipment, less efficient operation, and more pollution. We now have evidence that liberalized trade regimes lead to improved technology and greater efficiency and, with supportive environmental policies, improved environmental conditions. (Note that the *process* of liberalization may have some negative impact on the environment, but the *state* of undistorted trade incentives is almost certainly more pro-environment than distorted regimes.)

Clarifying property rights is another clearly pro-market and pro-environment policy. If squatters in urban slums are given legal title to their land, they will quadruple their investment in the local environment (sanitation, clean water, garbage disposal, and so on). If poor farmers in Africa who have no land rights are given such rights, the soil often stops deteriorating and starts improving. Why? Because the farmers start investing in simple soil-conservation techniques, and can use their land as collateral to borrow small amounts of money for the purpose. This effect is even dramatic when the property rights are given to *communities* rather than individuals. We have seen over-grazing reduced in the Sahel when communities of pastoralists were given rights and responsibilities of land ownership. And over-fishing in countries such as Sri Lanka has been reduced when local fishermen were given the task of allocating allowable catches among themselves.

But beyond this, what does the market do for the environment? The word "market" has been used in three senses in discussions about the environment, and this often creates confusion. The first refers to the *free market.* Does the free market solve environmental problems? The answer is partly yes, as discussed above, but largely no. Private factories, unregulated, will pollute not much less than public ones.

The second use of the phrase refers to *market instruments,* those instruments of policy designed to change behavior by providing graduated incentives rather than fixed standards. Effluent charges, carbon taxes, user charges, tradable permits, deposit-refund schemes, and performance bonds are examples of such instruments. Rightly used, these can allow great cost savings in a nation's efforts to reduce environmental damage. The early trading under the sulfur dioxide offset program illustrates the power of private initiative to figure out cheaper ways of doing things than public-sector bureaucrats. But for the present discussion, it is important to note that such market-based instruments are in a real sense just as "coercive" as command-and-control techniques. Government has to set either the *price* (the charge, tax, or fee) or the *quantity* (in the case of tradable permits). The market, left to itself, will not set both price and quantity in a manner that leads to a socially optimal outcome. Why? Because the environment that is damaged is fundamentally *external* to the market.

This leads to the third use of the word "market": the extension of excludable property rights to *all* natural assets—including water and air, even the upper atmosphere. If we were to extend property rights beyond the normal realm of such rights to *all* dimensions of environment, and do it in such a way that enforcement would be perfect and transaction costs minimal, we could, thanks to the Coase theorem, sleep soundly in the knowledge that environmental damage would be "optimal"!

This is of course an interesting conclusion, as many thousands of graduate students in environmental economics have discovered. But can we use it in any practical sense to argue that therefore "market" policies are better than coercive ones? Not really, unless we specify what we mean by the market. From a policy perspective the interest lies not in the abstract conclusion but in the details. Do free markets with "normal" property rights make coercion unnecessary? No, we need to supplement markets with a strong government. Should command-and-control policies be replaced with market-based instruments? Yes, to the extent possible, but we would still need a strong government to set such things as the volume of allowable pollution to be traded, or the fee to be charged for effluent. Should we move towards "extra-normal," all-embracing property rights? It would depend on how they were allocated and whether transaction costs could be kept down. And it would be necessary to have strong (and coercive) government indeed to decide who has the right to which part of the upper atmosphere!

Comments

James Nash: What P. J. Hill is doing is fundamentally cost-benefit analysis. This kind of analysis has some positive values, particularly when you are dealing with cost effectiveness. The problem is that cost-benefit analysis tends to reduce all moral values to market values. Moral values simply cannot be measured in terms of financial costs.

P. J. Hill also says that when the government has direct control over resources, the record is anything but good. I agree with some of what he says about the U.S. Forest Service and the Bureau of Reclamation, and I think I would add the Bureau of Land Management to this list. But I think there are some more positive possibilities. The national park system and the wildlife refuge system, though open to criticism on many points, have succeeded in preserving a variety of ecological values. Surely there are cases where government ownership has a chance to succeed.

P. J. Hill: Cost-benefit analysis does tend to reduce moral values to some sort of commercial values, and that is a very real problem. But trying to act upon moral values in the public-policy arena presents much the same sort of problem. We have to make policy trade-offs; Congress has to be involved in saying which sorts of values we want to deal with. There is a greater chance of retaining diversity of values, of allowing people to have preferences that are different from the prevailing wisdom and to act upon those, in a system of private property rights.

I agree that the national park system has preserved some resources and has in some cases done a good job. I have worked for the last

---

Note: These participants are identified on pages 151-52.

several years on Yellowstone National Park, however, and I am convinced that Yellowstone would have been much better preserved if we had allowed history to take its course. The Northern Pacific Railroad would have taken that area and managed it much better. Alston Chase's *Playing God in Yellowstone* is a very interesting summary of the bureaucratic mismanagement of the park. I agree that command and control can sometimes create a level playing field, but often what it means is that it diminishes the *size* of the playing field.

Andrew Steer: You *can* do cost-benefit analysis without putting monetary values on everything. The benefits of cleaner air come in the form of health dividends, productivity dividends, various amenities, and they may come in the form of intrinsic value. Including these in cost-benefit analysis is something we often haven't done.

Fred Smith: The first round of environmental action around the world dealt with big, relatively easy problems. Untreated sewage floating in rivers. Smokestacks belching large particulates. These were big, visible problems where even hamhanded governmental solutions could achieve relatively visible, significant effects. Now we are down to the smaller, more obscure problems. Which of the hundreds of small pollutants should we focus our efforts on? Andrew Steer has suggested two ways to decide: better science, and cost-benefit analysis. But the record of "better science" is abysmal. We spent $600 million in the United States assessing whether acid rain was a major problem or a minor problem. The National Acid Precipitation Assessment Program found that the threat was not as great and the costs were greater than we had thought. Congress tabled that study and passed the acid-rain bill anyway. Science has had little to do with environmental policy. Ron Bailey's book *Eco-Scam* and Michael Fumento's book *Science Under Siege* are replete with examples of where analysis failed to inform political decisions, despite our hopes. Politicians find it easier to base their vote on the sensational stories in the newspaper than on the dry analytic studies published in scientific journals. I don't see how politics can respond other than politically.

As for cost-benefit analysis: My first experience in the environmental area was with the Delaware River Basin Commission in the late seventies. How clean should we try to make the river? The commission suggested five options, ranging from 1, do nothing, to 5, close down Western civilization. The final decision was to make the river swimmable and clean enough to support shad, even though this was not cost-beneficial. The public works director of Philadelphia at the time pointed out that you could fly salmon in from Norway and put a swimming pool on every city block in Philadelphia for the cost of the cleanup. It didn't matter—politicians went ahead and approved the more costly solution. Cost-benefit analysis doesn't make politics go away.

The ability to protect a resource is not a given. A property-rights system requires that we be able to fence the land, and police it in some sense. But those abilities evolve in response to human need. The early American settlers knew about private property; they had had it in England. So when they landed in New England they built stone fences around their plots of land. Good fences make good neighbors. As they moved west and the stone supply played out, they built rail fences. But when they hit the great plains, two things changed: there was no stone and no wood, and the amount of land needed to maintain a viable family unit was thousands of acres. There was no feasible way of fencing property.

So what did the settlers do? They did the best they could in a world where fencing was impossible. They were trying to protect an environmental resource, the grass, and they had a pollutant, the cows. They branded the cows so they knew whose animals were eating whose grass. They created cattlemen's associations, which were essentially balancing agencies: if more of your cows ate my grass than my cows ate your grass, we made up the difference with side payments at the end of the year. An elaborate set of private police (cowboys) went around doing surveys to see whose pollutants were on whose properties. That system allowed us to produce a massive cattle industry in America. It was very costly. But because it was costly, it created incentives for people to come up with a better way. Barbed wire was the technological strategy that evolved in response to the need to do a better job of protecting an environmental resource.

We don't know what the barbed-wire equivalents are likely to be to protect the air, the water, the oceans, the fugitive wildlife of the world. But if we create the concept of decentralized private management, we encourage such better solutions to evolve. Modern tools such as satellite observation and DNA identification might well play a role here. If we want to better protect the environment, we must enlist private, decentralized incentive structures. Politics can't do that.

Andrew Steer: If we really want to talk about the evolution of property rights, we should talk about the evolution of rights to clean air. Should the developing world have a right to an upper atmosphere —which after all is above their countries—that will allow only so much sunlight to get through? Do they have a right to ozone in their upper atmosphere? Do they have a right to a reasonably low carbon content in their upper atmosphere so that they don't get greenhouse warming? Do I have a right to breathe clean air?

Fred Smith: No, you do not have a right to breathe clean air. You have a right to own air and you have a right to prevent people from putting things in your air.

Andrew Steer: How do I buy air over my house? How do you create an institution that enables me to have clean air over my house?

Fred Smith: We allow people to petition for control over the air in the jurisdiction that affects them, as we have done with watersheds in the past. We pass enabling legislation to let people homestead the air, the waters, the oceans.

Andrew Steer: That's the Clean Air Act.

Fred Smith: No, there is a tremendous difference between tradable rights to pollute, or licenses to pollute, and the right to determine how I will use the air in my backyard. Many, many goods in a voluntary world are not owned individually. The stores in a shopping mall don't own each little piece of the mall; the mall has both commonly owned areas and purely private areas.

Think about how property rights evolved in minerals beneath the surface of the earth. America created the modern mineral industry. How did we do it? We were the first country in the world that allowed people to own subsurface rights. Initially someone drilled a well down beneath his property, found oil, created a new industry. But because the oil field extended much further then the bounds of any single owner, there were externality problems. The property was badly segmented. This encouraged "unitization" strategies to develop that integrated the various subsurface rights into one unit. Now oil pools—not just oil wells—around the world are owned and managed privately. Creative airsheds-management approaches will emerge if we allow airshed property rights to exist. An individual would have the right to protect his or her airshed, but that right would best be managed by amalgamating such disparate individual rights into larger airshed districts and allowing the districts to negotiate with the various users and potential polluters to achieve a desired air quality. We're a long way from understanding the nuances of that. But the absolute unwillingness to look at these kinds of things is leaving us with the insanity of current environmental policy.

Ronald Bailey: What markets do very well is to create wealth. Creating wealth means we spend some of it in improving our environment. A lot of pollution curves were going steeply down in industrial countries well before there was a huge apparatus of pollution-control bureaucracies. That was happening voluntarily. People had gotten rich enough to say, I don't want to breathe this stuff anymore.

Andrew Steer: The traditional view is that as you get richer, the environment gets worse. As you get richer, you do put out more garbage. But some things get better as you get richer. Better sanitation. Cleaner water. And the notion that as you get richer you pollute more is dead wrong. The real relationship is more complicated. Paul Ehrlich says pollution is directly related to the scale of the economy: the bigger the economy, the worse the pollution. Yes, if all other things remain equal, then the more you produce, the more the pollution. But a lot of other things are going on at the same time. As you get richer you are willing to spend a lot more on pollution control. You also get a lot more efficient, so you save a lot of input.

Particulate matter is the most serious form of air pollution. It is very cheap to deal with; it costs 1 per cent of capital cost if you are building a power plant. So you deal with it straightaway because the health impact is very serious. The United States did it thirty years ago; China is doing it now. But dealing with sulfur dioxide is quite expensive: it costs up to 25 per cent of capital cost in some companies, and the benefits of reducing sulfur dioxide are not so great.

Robert Nelson: There are lots of forms of government failure, and one way government can fail is by trying to create property rights. Why is 30 per cent of the land in the United States publicly owned?

Because of government failure in property-rights creation. In the nineteenth century, the federal government was trying to dispose of all the public lands in the West. It devised an elaborate system of laws to do this, fully intending that by the year 1900 or 1910 the process would have been accomplished. It didn't happen. The laws were so bad, so poorly designed and administered, that a large part of the land never passed out of federal ownership.

People think the Homestead Act was one of the great successes of American history. Actually it was a major failure. The principle of homesteading had worked in midwestern states like Iowa, but that was when there was no Homestead Act and people simply went out and squatted. It took Congress about sixty years to decide that squatting wasn't an illegal infringement on the government's rights and should be recognized as a principle, and to devise a homestead law to transfer property rights and create a private-property regime. Unfortunately, by the time Congress passed the Homestead Act, settlement was moving out of Iowa and Kansas and Nebraska into places like Colorado and Nevada, where basically the 160 acres granted by the Act were enough to support a cow for a few months. One cow. For a viable ranching operation you needed something like 10,000-20,000 acres, and so the homestead law never worked. If we try to have institutions create property rights today, they may blunder just as badly.

With public property you don't necessarily get public ownership in the sense that the government attempts to manage the property in some generalized public interest. You may get interest groups competing for the use of the lands, for various forms of entitlements, some of which become in essence property rights. And it's not just ranchers with grazing rights—wilderness users are in a certain sense the property-rights holders to wilderness areas. The Wilderness Society has a lot more control over the management of a wilderness area than the Secretary of the Interior does.

On public lands, there are outfitter guide permits, boating permits, and so on to administer, and we get into an elaborate system. This can prove to be extremely expensive as a property-rights system. It's very cumbersome and can involve a lot of administrative costs. When I was at the Interior Department I did some calculations about grazing and came up with the estimate that if we were able to buy out all the grazing rights on public lands, it would cost about a billion dollars, whereas administrative costs to the federal government of livestock grazing on public lands in the future would add up to somewhere between two and four billion dollars.

Public lands also become areas where people get to experiment with their own theologies, their own ideas of what is most important. Yellowstone National Park had a policy that if mountain goats came into the park from the northeast or south side, everything possible would be done to get rid of them; if necessary they would be shot. But if mountain goats came in from the west side, the red carpet was rolled out for them. They were the same goats, having exactly the same impact on the park. The reason that the mountain goats from the west side were encouraged was that they were a natural population, while those on the northeast and south sides were introduced by hunters about 50-100 years ago. The same kind of idea in terms of elk management—the unwillingness to interfere with nature, the elevation of the idea that naturalness is a standard—is currently having an extremely destructive effect on Yellowstone Park. A lot of species are being driven off, while the elk have proliferated and have made a mess of the place.

With public lands, then, you may still get private property rights, you often get inefficient policies, and you get government officials sometimes being driven by fairly marginal viewpoints as they make decisions with a significant impact on the future of the land.

Richard Baer: I keep coming back to the thought that in 1790 our largest city, Philadelphia, had only 42,000 people; the sixth largest city, Salem, Massachusetts, had just under 8,000. People could talk about these issues and come to some community consensus. Today we are such a disparate conglomeration of people. Perhaps we need some forum in which to engage one another more openly, immune from market forces for a while. What does the land mean to us: does it have religious significance, symbolic meaning, historical meaning? Could we carry on such a discussion without letting it get as polarized as it usually does, with the nature types seeing market people as temple-destroyers and the market people seeing the nature types as woolly-headed dreamers?

James Nash: What comes to my mind is the historical concept in Christian ethics of the common good. A lot of the debate here has assumed basic positions on a dichotomy that might be called individualism versus communitarianism. In communitarian thought there is something called the common good that simply cannot be divided up. The air, the waters. Species. There are some things that ought to be preserved for the sake of the good we have in common.

Fred Smith: If I were a dogmatic Catholic in sixteenth-century Spain, that is exactly the line of argument I would advance: the common good demands one universal Catholic Church, and we must fight, if necessary, to advance that common good. America is heading toward eco-theocratic wars unless we find a way of depoliticizing environmental policy. Value resolution is easier outside the political realm. Politics is about conflict.

Charles Rubin: Some people approved of religious wars. They thought that certain values were worth fighting for, and that institutions that interfered with efforts to save souls or improve the human condition were bad ideas. Institutions are not value neutral; people can engage in conflict over institutional structures as well, in the environmental area as well as anywhere else.

Craig Rucker: On the public versus private issue: The American side of Niagara Falls is built right up to the brim with factories. It's terrible; nobody I know goes to the American side. The Canadian side is government-run, by and large. They do allow some private commercial enterprises, but the government sets limits to where the private sector can operate. It seems to me that we can preserve our parks, allow for private industry in certain areas, and yet retain our concern for cultural values.

Andrew Steer: But in many other parts of the world, government ownership has ruined things. Nepal is a good example. Communities used to manage all the forests. Twenty years ago the government decided that communities couldn't manage the forests, and it took over the whole responsibility. The forests were nearly ruined. Now they are being denationalized and given back to the communities. It all depends on the individual circumstances.

Richard Baer: The common good in some of these cases may be for the majority to admit there's not a consensus and decide to accommodate minorities on some of these issues when it's not too costly. Part of the genius of America is that we've allowed the Amish, Quakers, Native Americans, and others to be different where the cost has not been huge. Maybe there are some land cases where that's the model that might work best.

R. J. Smith: A senior official in one of the major conservation groups admitted that his group had supported the listing of the spotted owl as an endangered species not so much out of concern about the spotted owl but because they wanted to save the ancient forest and that was the only tool they had. Maybe the rules should be changed, so that, for example, when a forest sale comes up, not only can the timber-products company bid to chop down those trees, but the people who tell us that the trees are vital to them as a wilderness cathedral can bid to preserve them. A similar issue came up in Wisconsin, where some of the followers of Otto Leopold wanted to restore an area to the kind of condition it was in before the white man came there. One thing they wanted to do was reintroduce elk. Some grazing permits came up for sale, and they bid on them in order to raise elk. The government told them that they could not do that: you can get a grazing permit only to raise domestic livestock, not to graze elk or deer and not to retire the land from grazing. We might be able to find agreement on both sides of the fence to allow some competition on bids of this sort.

Privatizing a park or a wildlife refugee doesn't necessarily mean giving it to Exxon or Disneyland. Groups like the Audubon Society and the Nature Conservancy are also private organizations, and they both manage many extremely sensitive areas and some quite large ones. One of the Audubon Society's wildlife refuges is nearly 27,000 acres. In many of those places, not only are there no concession stands, but there's no way to get in there at all. The private organizations are preserving them perfectly, because they think that the areas are too sensitive to let the public in. That's far more difficult to do when you have 250 million taxpayers demanding the right to enter their parks.

There's a common belief that market demand caused the buffalo and the passenger pigeon to become extinct. But it wasn't market demand; it was the fact that there were no property rights in those resources. When market demand rose, everybody had an incentive to kill as many as he could, and nobody had an incentive to produce more. When the market demand for beef goes up, beef cattle don't become extinct; every rancher in the country produces beef as fast as he can. When the market demand for chicken goes up, Frank Perdue does not run out of chicken; he figures out how to get his chickens to produce more chickens as fast as possible. The key issue is property rights.

APPENDIX

Conference Participants

Richard Baer, Jr., professor of environmental ethics, Cornell University.

Ronald Bailey, executive producer, New River Media.

Peter Bakken, research associate, Au Sable Institute of Environmental Studies.

Michael Cromartie, senior fellow, Ethics and Public Policy Center.

Thomas Sieger Derr, chair, Department of Religion and Biblical Literature, Smith College.

Susan Drake, international coral reef initiative coordinator, Department of State.

Christopher Flavin, vice-president, Worldwatch Institute.

Peter J. Hill, professor of economics, Wheaton College.

Andrew Kimbrell, director, International Center for Technology Assessment.

Jo Kwong, environmental research associate, Atlas Economic Research Foundation.

Richard Land, executive director, Christian Life Commission, Southern Baptist Convention.

Stan LeQuire, director, Evangelical Environmental Network.

Patrick J. Michaels, associate professor of environmental sciences, University of Virginia.

James A. Nash, executive director, Churches' Center for Theology and Public Policy.

Robert Nelson, professor of environmental policy, University of Maryland.

Robert Royal, vice-president, Ethics and Public Policy Center.

Charles T. Rubin, associate professor of political science, Duquesne University.

Craig Rucker, executive director, Committee for a Constructive Tomorrow.

Ronald Sider, president, Evangelicals for Social Action.

Fred Smith, president, Competitive Enterprise Institute.

R. J. Smith, senior environmental scholar, Competitive Enterprise Institute.

Andrew Steer, director, Environment Department, The World Bank.

Michael Uhlmann, senior fellow, Ethics and Public Policy Center.

Robert Vashon, senior scientist for environmental public policy, Procter and Gamble.

George Weigel, president, Ethics and Public Policy Center.

Richard Wright, chair, Division of Natural Sciences and Mathematics, Gordon College.

Notes

CHAPTER 1

"Managing the Planet"

CHARLES T. RUBIN

1. William D. Ruckelshaus, "Risk, Science and Democracy," *Issues in Science and Technology* 1 (Spring 1985): 25.

2. For an excellent overview and discussion of the various schools of thought on this point, see David Dery, *Problem Definition in Policy Analysis* (Lawrence: University Press of Kansas, 1984), 14-27.

3. Charles T. Rubin, *The Green Crusade: Rethinking the Roots of Environmentalism* (New York: The Free Press, 1994).

4. Compare, for example, Penelope ReVelle and Charles ReVelle, *The Environment: Issues and Choices for Society* (Boston: Jones and Bartlett, 1988), and Bernard J. Nebel, *Environmental Science: The Way the World Works,* 3d ed. (Englewood Cliffs: Prentice Hall, 1990), 576.

5. Barry Commoner, *The Closing Circle: Nature, Man and Technology* (New York: Knopf, 1971), 33.

6. Paul R. Ehrlich and John P. Holdren, "Impact of Population Growth," *Science* 171 (March 1971): 1215, 1212.

7. Zygmunt J. B. Plater et al., *Environmental Law and Policy: Nature, Law and Society* (St. Paul: West Publishing Co., 1992), 597 [Public Law 91-190 (1970)].

8. Roger W. Findley and Daniel A. Farber, eds., *Cases and Materials on Environmental Law,* 3d ed. (St. Paul: West Publishing Co., 1991), 110.

9. Eugene C. Hargrove, ed., *Beyond Spaceship Earth: Environmental Ethics and the Solar System* (San Francisco: Sierra Club Books, 1986).

10. William H. Rodgers, *Environmental Law* (St. Paul: West Publishing Co., 1977), 1.

11. Lynton Keith Caldwell, *International Environmental Policy: Emergence and Dimensions,* 2d ed. (Durham: Duke University Press, 1990), 7.

12. R. Cowen, "Vanishing Amphibians: Why They're Croaking," *Science News* 137 (February 24, 1990): 116.

13. Richard John Neuhaus, *In Defense of People: Ecology and the Seduction of Radicalism* (New York: Macmillan, 1971), 112-13.

14. See, for example, Dolores LaChapelle, *Earth Wisdom* (Silverton: Finn Hill Arts, 1978), 45-49.

15. Garrett Hardin, *The Limits of Altruism: An Ecologist's View of Survival* (Bloomington: Indiana University Press, 1977), 56-57.

16. Thomas Berry, *The Dream of the Earth* (San Francisco: Sierra Club Books, 1988), 29.

17. Ibid., 27.

18. Ibid., 66.

19. Ibid., 4.

20. Ibid., 25, 27.

21. Ibid., 30.

22. Ibid., 41.

23. Ibid.

24. Scientific American, *Managing Planet Earth* (New York: W. H. Freeman, 1990).

25. World Commission on Environment and Development, *Our Common Future* (Oxford: Oxford University Press, 1987), 46.

26. Paul Lewis, "Storm in Rio: Morning After," *New York Times,* June 15, 1992 (National Edition), 1.

27. Edward O. Wilson, *The Diversity of Life* (Cambridge: Harvard University Press, 1992), 312-19.

28. Paul R. Ehrlich, *The Population Bomb* (New York: Ballantine Books, 1968), 75.

29. Karen F. Schmidt, "Dioxin's Other Face," *Science News* 141 (January 11, 1992): 24.

30. Al Gore, *Earth in the Balance: Ecology and the Human Spirit* (New York: Penguin Books, 1993), 29.

31. Ibid., 177, 295ff.

32. Ibid., 232-34, 301-2. Gore is not beyond moral equivalence: both capitalist and totalitarian societies are analogized to dysfunctional families. His confusion on totalitarianism is indicated by his willingness to make the environment "the central organizing principle for civilization" (269).

33. Ibid., 272.

34. Winston S. Churchill, *The World Crisis 1911-1918* (New York: Barnes and Noble, 1993), 1131.

35. Elizabeth Pennisi, "Conservation's Ecocentrics," *Science News* 144 (September 11, 1993): 170.

36. Martin W. Lewis, *Green Delusions: An Environmentalist Critique of Radical Environmentalism* (Durham: Duke University Press, 1992), 37.

37. Ehrlich, *Population Bomb,* 15.

38. William Devall, *Simple in Means, Rich in Ends: Practicing Deep Ecology* (Salt Lake City: Gibbs Smith, 1988), 39.

39. Marvin Minsky, "Will Robots Inherit the Earth?," *Scientific American,* October 1994, 113.

40. Hans Moravec, *Mind Children: The Future of Robot and Human Intelligence* (Cambridge: Harvard University Press, 1988), 1.

41. Rene Dubos, *The Wooing of Earth: New Perspectives on Man's Use of Nature* (New York: Scribner, 1980), 109-10.

42. Rene Dubos, *Celebrations of Life* (New York: McGraw-Hill, 1981), 83.

43. Compare David E. Cooper, "The Idea of Environment," in David E. Cooper and Joy A. Palmer, eds., *The Environment in Question* (London: Routledge, 1992), 165-80. This essay is an extremely thoughtful argument along the lines of the one presented here, although with a narrower focus. It is directed particularly against those who call for a "'new' environmental ethic" (165). "Put crudely, their notion of environment is of something much too big" (167). Cooper regards this usage, which he calls "The Environment," as a departure from an earlier employment of the term, which was limited to "something for a creature, a field of meanings or significance" (169). "New" ethics that ask us to feel oneness with or reverence for The Environment are incoherent because they attempt to extend such sentiments into a realm where they are inappropriate, and because The Environment is a result of the very scientific thinking the new ethics so often rail against. Cooper doubts that any new environmental ethic is necessary and suggests that people would best focus on what is close to them if they care about their relationship to the environment.

A crucial flaw mars this otherwise lovely essay. In commending a concept of the environment as field of significance, and in turning however briefly to Martin Heidegger to bolster that case, Cooper neglects the lesson Heidegger teaches: that such fields are not given to human beings once and for all. For Heidegger, it is only too likely that (in Cooper's terms) we will come to understand our field of significance as The Environment, however destructive that might be to something that is (in ways that remain mysterious) more genuinely human. If that is happening or should happen, then it seems likely that a new ethic would be necessary. Cooper, it seems unwittingly, himself provides evidence for the seductions of such a change as he at one moment (quite rightly) discusses how the concept of sustainable development glosses over the issue of "depriving people of environments which are the setting for the traditional activities in which they are 'at home'" (174), and at the next moment presents his personal experience of being one day anchored off the coast of Egypt and the next day back in his "personal, homely" realm of pine woods (177).

To put what is essentially the same point another way, Cooper does not pay the attention he should to how often those authors who he believes display a proper understanding of environment speak not in the language of environment at all but about nature.

Response by ANDREW KIMBRELL

1. Charles T. Rubin, *The Green Crusade* (New York: The Free Press, 1994), 173.

2. E. F. Schumacher, *Good Work* (New York: Harper & Row, 1979).

3. "Toward a Human Scale Technology," in Schumacher, *Good Work,* 23.

4. See Rubin, *The Green Crusade,* 55, n. 34.

5. Samuel P. Hays, *Conservation and the Gospel of Efficiency* (New York: Atheneum, 1979).

6. George Dalton, ed., *Primitive, Archaic and Modern Economies: Essays of Karl Polanyi* (Boston: Beacon Press, 1968), 62.

CHAPTER 2

"The Climate-Change Debacle"
PATRICK J. MICHAELS

1. S. Manabe et al., "Transient Responses of a Coupled Ocean-Atmosphere Model to Gradual Changes of Atmospheric CO_2: Part One: Annual Mean Response," *Journal of Climate* 4 (1991): 785-818.

2. R. C. Balling and S. B. Idso, "100 Years of Global Warming?," *Environmental Conservation* 17 (1990): 165.

3. Ibid.

4. Intergovernmental Panel on Climate Change, "Scientific Assessment of Climate Change" (U.N. Environment Programme, 1990).

5. Manabe, "Transient Responses."

6. J. C. Rogers, Proceedings, 13th Annual Climate Diagnostics Workshop (U.S. Department of Commerce, 1989).

7. J. Samson, "Antarctic Surface Temperature Time Series," *Journal of Climate* 2 (1989): 1164-72.

8. J. D. Kahl et al., "Absence of Evidence for Greenhouse Warming Over the Arctic Ocean in the Past Forty Years," *Nature* 361 (1993): 335-37.

9. L. S. Kalkstein, T. C. Dunne, and R. S. Vose, "Detection of Climatic Change in the Western North American Arctic Using a Synoptic Climatological Approach," *Journal of Climate* 3 (1990): 1154-67.

10. T. M. L. Wigley, "Could Reducing Fossil-Fuel Emissions End Global Warming?," *Nature* 349 (1991): 503-5; R. J. Charlson et al., "Climate Forcing by Anthropogenic Aerosols," *Science* 225 (1992): 423-30.

11. Patrick J. Michaels, D. C. Knappenberger, and D. A. Gay, "General Circulation Models: Testing the Forecast," *Technology: Journal of the Franklin Institute* 331A (1994): 123-33.

12. J. E. Hansen, M. Sato, and R. Ruedy, "Long-Term Changes of the Diurnal Temperature Cycle: Implications About Mechanisms of Global Climate Change," U.S. Department of Energy Conf. 9309350, 1993, 313-25.

Response by CHRISTOPHER FLAVIN

1. Intergovernmental Panel on Climate Change, "IPCC Second Scientific Assessment," draft, Zurich, 1994.

2. The Hadley Centre, *Modelling Climate Change* (Bracknell, U.K., 1995).

3. Charles Petit, "New Hints of Global Warming," *San Francisco Chronicle,* April 17, 1995.

4. David J. Thomson, "The Seasons, Global Temperature, and Precession," *Science,* April 7, 1995.

5. William K. Stevens, "More Extremes Found in Weather, Pointing to Greenhouse Gas Effect," *New York Times,* May 23, 1995.

6. Charles Petit, "New Hints of Global Warming," *San Francisco Chronicle,* April 17, 1995.

7. Ibid.

8. George M. Woodwell and Fred T. Mackenzie, *Biotic Feedbacks in the Global*

Climatic System: Will the Warming Feed the Warming? (New York: Oxford University Press, 1995).

9. Walter Sullivan, "New Theory on Ice Sheet Catastrophe Is the Direst One Yet," *New York Times,* May 2, 1995.

10. Swiss Reinsurance Company, *Global Warming: Element of Risk* (Zurich, 1994).

11. Christopher Flavin and Nicholas Lenssen, *Power Surge: A Guide to the Coming Energy Revolution* (New York: W. W. Norton, 1994).

CHAPTER 4

"The Challenge of Biocentrism"

THOMAS SIEGER DERR

1. Lynn White, Jr., "The Historical Roots of Our Ecologic Crisis," *Science,* 155 (March 10, 1967): 1203-7.

2. George Sessions, "Introduction" (to Part II, "Deep Ecology"), in Michael Zimmerman, ed., *Environmental Philosophy: From Animal Rights to Radical Ecology* (Englewood Cliffs, N.J.: Prentice Hall, 1993), 161.

3. Paul Ehrlich and Richard L. Harriman, *How to Be a Survivor* (New York: Ballantine, 1971), 129.

4. Alfred North Whitehead, *Science and the Modern World* (New York: Macmillan, 1950 [original 1925]).

5. Lynn White, "Continuing the Conversation," in Ian G. Barbour, ed., *Western Man and Environmental Ethics* (Reading, Mass.: Addison-Wesley, 1973). Also private conversations.

6. Douglas John Hall, *The Steward: A Biblical Symbol Come of Age* (Grand Rapids: Eerdmans, 1990). Loren Wilkinson et al., *Earthkeeping in the Nineties: Stewardship of Creation* (Grand Rapids: Eerdmans, 1991). Derr, *Ecology and Human Need* (Philadelphia: Westminster, 1973 and 1975).

7. Rene Dubos, *A God Within* (New York: Scribner, 1972), 161. See pp. 157-61 for his argument against White's thesis.

8. Clarence Glacken, *Traces on the Rhodian Shore: Nature and Culture in Western Thought from Ancient Times to the End of the Eighteenth Century* (Berkeley: University of California, 1967), 423.

9. Richard Sylvan, "Is There a Need for a New, an Environmental Ethic?" in Zimmerman, *Environmental Philosophy,* 13-14.

10. Paul Taylor, "The Ethics of Respect for Nature," in Zimmerman, *Environmental Philosophy,* 78-80.

11. Biocentrists and animal-rights activists are further and seriously separated by the former's focus on saving individuals, and the latter's giving priority to species. A biocentrist, who is indifferent to suffering in the wild (just part of the natural ecosystem, which is good), would allow, even encourage, the death of weaker individuals so that the species as a whole may flourish. For this a leading animal-rights advocate, Tom Regan, has fastened upon biocentrism the charming sobriquet "ecofascism" (*The Case for Animal Rights* [Berkeley: University of California, 1983], 262). But biocentrists reject this "humanitarian ethic" as misplaced in nature. It is not a true

"environmental ethic." Thus Mark Sagoff: "Mother Nature is so cruel to her children she makes Frank Perdue look like a saint" ("Animal Liberation and Environmental Ethics: Bad Marriage, Quick Divorce," in Zimmerman, *Environmental Philosophy,* 89-92).

12. Not all biocentrists reject the argument from defective human beings, however. Kenneth Goodpaster uses it to deny that "moral considerability" should be restricted to humans because they are rational. He extends moral status beyond humans, and beyond animals, too, to all that is alive ("On Being Morally Considerable," in Zimmerman, *Environmental Philosophy,* 54, 56).

13. Systematically in Holmes Rolston, *Environmental Ethics: Duties to and Values in the Natural World* (Philadelphia: Temple University Press, 1988).

14. Ibid., 9.

15. Ibid., 100.

16. Ibid., 112-16.

17. James A. Nash, *Loving Nature: Ecological Integrity and Christian Responsiblity* (Nashville: Abingdon, 1991), 99. See also his essay "Biotic Rights and Human Ecological Responsibility," in *The Annual of the Society of Christian Ethics, 1993,* 137-62.

18. Rolston, *Environmental Ethics,* 218.

19. Ibid., 240-41.

20. Nash, *Loving Nature,* 176, 181; "Biotic Rights," 150-51, 158-59. Nash would not award rights to abiotic entities, only organisms; and thus he rejects the term "rights of nature," though granting, like Rolston, that "the term remains rhetorically valuable" ("Biotic Rights," 148).

21. Rolston, *Environmental Ethics,* 48.

22. Ibid., 50-51.

23. Larry Rasmussen's phrase, defending the extension of neighbor love even to inorganic nature; in Wesley Granberg-Michaelson, ed., *Tending the Garden: Essays on the Gospel and the Earth* (Grand Rapids: Eerdmans, 1987), 199. For an anti-theological version of the extension argument, see J. Baird Callicott, following his hero, the much-cited Aldo Leopold, *In Defense of the Land Ethic* (Albany: State University of New York, 1989), 80-82.

24. H. Paul Santmire, *The Travail of Nature: The Ambiguous Ecological Promise of Christian Theology* (Philadelphia: Fortress, 1985). Nash, *Loving Nature,* 124-33.

25. Arne Naess, "The Deep Ecological Movement: Some Philosophical Aspects," in Zimmerman, *Environmental Philosophy,* 203. George Sessions is less severe but, as a "biocentric egalitarian," will give us no more than equality with nature: non-human entities have "equal inherent value or worth along with humans" ("Deep Ecology and Global Ecosystem Protection," in Zimmerman, *Environmental Philosophy,* 236).

26. Rolston, *Environmental Ethics,* 155. That is not, strictly speaking, quite true. Nature has a way of restoring devastated land, whether it be laid waste by a volcano or an atomic bomb test. Extinction of species on a grand scale is simply the way of nature, and always has been, since well before human life appeared.

27. Rolston, *Environmental Ethics,* 103.

28. Hardin's essay "The Tragedy of the Commons" (*Science,* December 13, 1968) is still routinely cited and anthologized, as are the conclusions he drew from it in another essay, "Living on a Lifeboat" (*Bioscience* 24, 1974). But harshest of all is *Exploring New Ethics for Survival: The Voyage of the Spaceship Beagle* (Baltimore: Penguin, 1973), which is virtually invisible today. The quotation from William Aiken is from

his essay "Ethical Issues in Agriculture," in Tom Regan, ed., *Earthbound: New Introductory Essays in Environmental Ethics* (New York: Random House, 1984), 269; cited in Callicott, *In Defense of the Land Ethic,* 92. This is not Aiken's position, though Callicott's alterations make it appear to be so. Aiken says that these statements, which in his essay are questions, would be those of a position he calls "eco-holism," an extreme stance that he suggests may be ascribed to Paul Taylor among others, and which he rejects in favor of a more humanistic one. On p. 272 he outlines a scale of comparative value much like Nash's, one that favors human beings.

29. Lynn White, "The Future of Compassion," *The Ecumenical Review* 30, no. 2 (April 1978): 108.

30. Rolston, *Environmental Ethics,* 329; Rolston, "Challenges in Environmental Ethics," in Zimmerman, *Environmental Philosophy,* 136; Nash, "Biotic Rights," 159; Callicott, *In Defense of the Land Ethic,* 93-94.

31. Taylor, "Ethics of Respect for Nature," 71, 81. Berry, in Zimmerman, *Environmental Philosophy,* 174.

32. Carol Christ, "Rethinking Theology and Nature," in Irene Diamond and Gloria Feman Orenstein, eds., *Reweaving the World: The Emergence of Ecofeminism* (San Francisco: Sierra Club, 1990), 68.

33. Rolston, *Environmental Ethics,* 185-86, 195-98 (quoting in part P. C. W. Davies).

34. Ibid., 344-45.

35. James Gustafson, *A Sense of the Divine: The Natural Environment from a Theocentric Perspective* (Cleveland: Pilgrim Press [forthcoming]), chaps. 1 and 3 in the unpaginated ms. Nash, *Loving Nature,* 233-34, n. 10, commenting on Gustafson's *Theocentric Ethics,* vol. 1 (Chicago: University of Chicago Press, 1981), 106, 183-84, 248-50, 270-73.

36. Michael Zimmerman, "Deep Ecology and Ecofeminism: The Emerging Dialogue," in Diamond and Orenstein, *Reweaving the World,* 140. Zimmerman, like Naess and Sessions, is a "biocentric egalitarian"; thus: "Humanity is no more, but also no less, important than all other things on earth" (ibid.).

Response by JAMES A. NASH

1. James A. Nash, *Loving Nature: Ecological Integrity and Christian Responsibility* (Nashville: Abingdon Press, 1991), 22.

2. See Nash, *Loving Nature,* chap. 3.

3. Ibid., chaps. 4-5.

4. Michael Freeden, *Rights* (Minneapolis: University of Minnesota Press, 1991), 61, 64.

5. Nash, *Loving Nature,* chap. 7; James A. Nash, "Biotic Rights and Human Ecological Responsibility," in Harlan Beckley, ed., *The Annual of the Society of Christian Ethics, 1993* (Boston: SCE, 1993), 137-62; and James A. Nash "The Case for Biotic Rights," *Yale Journal of International Law* 18, no. 1 (1993): 235-49.

6. James A. Nash, "Human Rights and the Environment: New Challenge for Ethics," *Theology and Public Policy* 4, no. 2 (Fall 1992): 42-57.

7. On eco-justice, see especially Dieter T. Hessel, ed., *After Nature's Revolt: Eco-justice and Theology* (Minneapolis: Fortress Press, 1992). See also the annotated entries in "Ecology, Justice, and Christian Faith: A Guide to the Literature, 1960-93," compiled by Peter W. Bakken, J. Ronald Engel, and Joan Gibb Engel (forthcoming).

CHAPTER 5

"Can Markets or Government Do More for the Environment?"

PETER J. HILL

1. U.S. Forest Service, Timber Sale Program Annual Report (Washington, D.C.: U.S. Forest Service, 1989), 8-9.

2. Utah Foundation, *The Utah Foundation Research Report* #572 (July 1994), 293-304.

3. Delworth B. Gardner and Ray G. Huffaker, "Cutting the Losses from Federal Water Subsidies," *Choices,* Fourth Quarter 1988, 24-26.

4. See, for instance: Mark Maremont, Jonathan Kapstein, and Gail E. Schares, "Eastern Europe's Big Cleanup," *Business Week,* March 19, 1990, 114-15; Phillip P. Micklin, "Desiccation of the Aral Sea: A Water Management Disaster in the Soviet Union," *Science* 241 (Sept. 1, 1988): 1170-76; Frederick Painton, "Where the Sky Stays Dark," *Time,* May 28, 1990, 40-42.

5. Frances Cairncross, *Costing the Earth: The Challenge for Governments, the Opportunities for Business* (Boston: Harvard Business School Press, 1992), 60-61.

6. Robert Crandall and John Graham, "The Politics of Energy: New Fuel-Economy Standards?," *The American Enterprise,* March/April 1991.

7. For a discussion of the debate over the best way to reduce sulfur oxides see: Bruce A. Ackerman and W. T. Hassler, *Clean Coal/Dirty Air, or How the Clean-Air Act Became a Multibillion-Dollar Bailout for High Sulfur Coal Producers and What Should Be Done About It* (New Haven: Yale University Press, 1981).

8. For a discussion of how politics warped the Clean Air Act Amendments, see Jonathan Adler, "Clean Fuels, Dirty Air: How a (Bad) Bill Became Law," *The Public Interest* 108 (Summer 1992): 116-31.

9. Terry L. Anderson, *Water Crisis: Ending the Policy Drought* (Baltimore: Johns Hopkins University Press, 1983).

10. *The Economist,* "A Sustainable Stock of Fisherman," January 19, 1991, 17-18.

11. William L. Robinson, "Individual Transferable Quotas in the Australian Southern Bluefin Tuna Fishery," in Fishery Access Control Programs: Worldwide Proceedings of the Workshop in Management Options for the North Pacific Longline Fishers, Alaska Sea Grant Report 86-4 (Orcus Island, WA: University of Alaska, 1986), 186-205.

12. Anglers' Cooperative Association, pamphlet (Midland Bank Chambers, Grantham, Lincolnshire NG31 6LE, United Kingdom).

13. Mark Crawford, "Scientists Battle Over Grand Canyon Pollution," *Science* 247 (Feb. 23, 1990): 911-12.

Index of Names